PENGUIN BOOKS

TIME WILL WRITE A SONG FOR YOU

Kannan M. (b. 1968) heads the Programme on Contemporary Tamil Culture, Department of Indology, French Institute of Pondicherry.

Rebecca Whittington (b. 1987) is a PhD student in the Department of South and Southeast Asian Studies at the University of California, Berkeley. Her research interests include Tamil and Bengali modern literature, comparative literature, literary modernism, and translation studies.

D. Senthil Babu (b. 1972) is a historian of science affiliated to the Department of Indology, French Institute of Pondicherry.

David C. Buck (b. 1948) has been translating Tamil works into English since 1965. He has also studied Cittar and Saiva religion and philosophy, as well as Carnatic music on the veena. His publications include a number of collaborations with the late Dr K. Paramasivam, including a translation of *Iraiyanar Akapporul* with Nakkirar's commentary, as well as some Sangam poetry. He has also published a translation, with comments, of *Thirukkurraalak Kuravanci*. More recently, he has published a number of translations from contemporary Tamil literature in collaboration with Kannan M. of the French Institute in Pondicherry. David C. Buck is an Associate Professor Emeritus at Elizabethtown Community and Technical College in Kentucky, USA.

TIME *will write* A SONG *for you*

Contemporary Tamil Writing from Sri Lanka

Edited and translated by Kannan M., Rebecca Whittington, D. Senthil Babu, David C. Buck

FRENCH INSTITUTE OF PONDICHERRY

PENGUIN BOOKS

An imprint of Penguin Random House

PENGUIN BOOKS

USA | Canada | UK | Ireland | Australia
New Zealand | India | South Africa | China | Singapore

Penguin Books is part of the Penguin Random House group of companies whose addresses can be found at global.penguinrandomhouse.com

Published by Penguin Random House India Pvt. Ltd
4th Floor, Capital Tower 1, MG Road,
Gurugram 122 002, Haryana, India

First published by Penguin Books India in association with French Institute of Pondicherry 2014

Series: Regards sur l'Asie du Sud/South Asian Perspectives, No. 5, French Institute of Pondicherry

10 9 8 7 6 5 4 3 2

ISBN 9780143423041

Typeset in Dante MT Std by Eleven Arts, Delhi
Printed at Manipal Technologies Limited, India

www.penguin.co.in

Contents

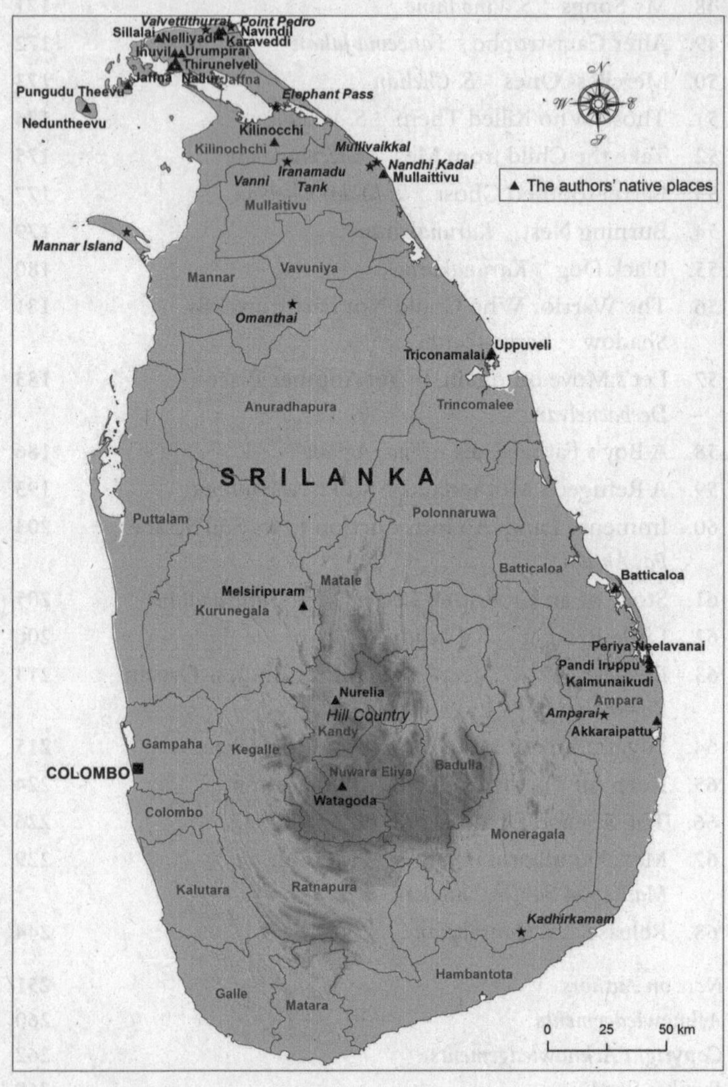
Valvettithurrai
Point Pedro
Sillalai
Nelliyadi
Navindil
Karaveddi
Inuvil
Urumpirai
Thirunelveli
Jaffna
Nallur
Jaffna
Pungudu Theevu
Neduntheevu
Elephant Pass
Kilinocchi
Kilinochchi
Mullivaikkal
Nandhi Kadal
Mullaittivu
Iranamadu Tank
Vanni
Mullaitivu
The authors' native places
Mannar Island
Mannar
Vavuniya
Omanthai
Uppuveli
Triconamalai
Anuradhapura
Trincomalee
S R I L A N K A
Puttalam
Polonnaruwa
Batticaloa
Batticaloa
Melsiripuram
Matale
Kurunegala
Periya Neelavanai
Pandi Iruppu
Kalmunaikudi
Nurelia
Ampara
Hill Country
Amparai
Kandy
Akkaraipattu
Gampaha
Kegalle
Badulla
COLOMBO
Nuwara Eliya
Watagoda
Colombo
Moneragala
Kalutara
Ratnapura
Kadhirkamam
Hambantota
Galle
Matara
0
25
50 km

Introduction

Walking on my bare knees
Through a field of broken glass /
Walking on my naked soul
Through a field of broken comrades /
. . .
Of death / killed /
By bullets or cyanide / by
Their own or another's hand / dead
All the same / rotting
. . .

Juan Gelman[1]

A Landscape and Its People

The words 'Tamil Writing from Sri Lanka'—part of the subtitle of this anthology—may invite critical discussion. Some people may say why *Sri Lanka*, why not *Tamil Ealam*? To understand this response, we have to engage with the concerns of the diverse Tamils in Sri Lanka, their roots and journey, especially over the past century and a half.

A teardrop in the Indian Ocean, the island's geopolitical location (its proximity to India and particularly Tamil Nadu) has made it a playground for the 'superpowers' operating in the region—India, China and the US. Tamils in Sri Lanka, constituting 18 per cent of

[1] Note III, in *Dark Times Filled with Light: The Selected Work of Juan Gelman*, translated from the Spanish by Hardie St Martin, Open Letter, Rochester, New York, 2012, p. 75.

the population, form the main minority, and live primarily in the northern and eastern regions and in the hills of the central region. Most hill-country Tamils are descended from indentured labourers brought from South India to work on British-owned tea plantations in central Sri Lanka during the era of British rule. There is a sharp distinction made between the 'Sri Lankan Tamils' descended from a community of people who have lived on the island for centuries, and the hill-country labourers. The ancient name for the parts of Sri Lanka populated mainly by Tamil-speaking people is *Ealam*. The majority Sinhalese-speaking population (74 per cent) lives in the lower central, western and southern parts of the island. Though these communities historically have been living in distinct regions within the island, they share a subcontinental religious culture, rooted in both classical and folk traditions. Further, the Tamil population itself is anything but monochromatic: besides the Sri Lankan versus hill-country division noted above, there are religion-based divisions as well. While most are Hindu, there are also many Christian Tamils and many Tamil-speaking Muslims, who live in geographically and culturally distinct regions. The major areas populated mainly by the Tamils include the Jaffna peninsula, which is the northernmost region of the island, and just to its south the Vanni, comprising the districts of Killinocchi, Mannar, Vavuniya and Mullaittivu, and the eastern coastal region centred on Triconamalai, Batticaloa and Ambarai. These communities all speak different, but mutually intelligible, dialects of Tamil, and all share in the same Tamil literary tradition.

As in India, the Tamils here are mired in hierarchies of caste and region as seen in Mahakavi's iconic poem, 'The Temple Car and the Moon'. The caste system of the Tamils here is however distinct from that of the Tamil region in India in that there has been no Brahmin hegemony. There has, however, existed a Saiva Vellala hegemony that aped the Brahmins, and has constituted its own hierarchy of lesser castes and untouchables. Regionalism among the Tamils of Sri Lanka has been sustained by the animated dominance of Jaffna, often considered the cultural capital of the Tamils, and the corresponding resentment and opposition towards it from other regions. Every other regional and caste group among the Tamils in Sri Lanka has notoriously looked down on the hill-country Tamils and considered them as yet another population of untouchables. There are other minorities, including certain tribal communities, which live in different regions of Sri Lanka.

People and their Struggle

The root cause of the struggle between the minority and the majority in Sri Lanka is the majoritarian attitude of many Sinhalese Buddhists, who are practitioners of Theravada Buddhism. An Act passed in 1956 made Sinhalese the single official language of Sri Lanka (then Ceylon), thereby practically forcing the minorities into a second-order citizenship soon after independence in 1948. The two decades that followed the passing of this Act witnessed significant political turbulence that in more ways than one, sowed the seeds of the conflict to come later. Within the Tamil community, these years were characterized by the emergence of strong working-class movements led by the Communist party. The Communists, with their belief in organizing an all-Sri Lankan working class, found it important to address issues of caste oppression within the Tamil community. They led several agitations and propaganda campaigns against caste oppression—in particular, against untouchability and the denial of basic rights like access to education, water and places of worship, to the oppressed sections. The Tamil nationalist parties, with their belief in parliamentary democracy, chose to frame their politics within a language of political rights, regional autonomy and democratic federalism vis-à-vis the Sri Lankan state. In 1964, a pact signed by Sirimavo Bandaranaike, then Sri Lankan prime minister, and Lal Bahadur Shastri,[2] her Indian counterpart, forced lakhs of disenfranchised Tamil indentured labourers living in the central hills to return to India, where they continue to live like refugees, isolated in a few hill stations, still finding it difficult to cope with the vagaries of resettlement. Those who managed to stay back faced severe hardship on the plantations, as they were harassed by their Sinhalese neighbours. As for those who resettled in other Tamil regions of the island, they faced even worse harassment at the hands of the dominant Tamil castes. Despite the serious injustice committed to lakhs of Tamil labourers, both the Tamil nationalists and the Communists staged merely token protests and continued with their set agenda. The political and social schisms within the Tamil community in the decades after 1956 prevented them from forging a unified political movement in the face of increasingly oppressive, majoritarian policies of the state of Ceylon.

In 1971, the Government of Ceylon implemented the so-called 'policy of standardization', which in effect curtailed the entry of Tamils into institutions of higher education and recruitment into government service. The proclamation of Sri Lanka as a republic in 1972 and the pride of place that Buddhism as a religion acquired in its Constitution further aggravated the tensions between the two communities. The Tamil people deeply resented such policies and perceived them as clear acts of discrimination against their culture and their legitimate status within the Sri Lankan nation. It was

---

[2] There were almost 10 lakh Tamils in the plantations at the time of signing the agreement. India was supposed to take back 5.25 lakh of people. The remaining 3 lakh people were assured Sri Lankan citizenship. The fate of the remaining 1.5 lakh Tamils in the hills was to be decided at a later date. The 5.25 lakh Tamils were supposed to leave Sri Lankan soil within fifteen years from the date of signing the agreement in batches of 36,000 per year. The Sri Lankan government was supposed to guarantee citizenship to 20,000 Tamils every year.

in such a situation that the fourth World Tamil Conference was held in Jaffna in 1974, much against the wishes of the Sri Lankan government, which preferred the national capital Colombo as the venue for the event. The rally on the last day of the conference was charged by the Sri Lankan police, who opened fire, causing the death of nine Tamils. (Iravi Arunasalam's 'A Story Lost in Time, Lasting in Time' has echoes of the event.)

These were the circumstances that animated the Tamil youth, disappointed with both the Tamil nationalist leadership and the Communist parties, whose politics did not seem to deliver hoped-for results. The events following the 1968 global uprisings and the strong emergence of the Naxalite movement in India inspired large sections of the Tamil youth to take a militant path to secure their rights: at best, a Tamil nation; or at least, an autonomous region within the Sri Lankan state. The struggle of the people of Palestine under the Palestine Liberation Organization (PLO) was an inspiration as well.[3] To contend with these sentiments of such a significant section of the Tamil youth, the Tamil nationalist parties convened a conference at Vattukkottai in 1976, where they passed a resolution demanding a full-fledged *Tamil Ealam*, nothing short of a Tamil homeland.

The 'self-appointed' President of Sri Lanka, J.R. Jayawardane, riding on a popular victory in the general elections of 1977, launched a direct attack against the Tamil nationalist leadership in the Sri Lankan Parliament, who were protesting against the police brutality in Jaffna. This provoked widespread attacks by Sinhalese gangs against the Tamil people all over Sri Lanka, resulting in

---

[3] Some of the early militants were indeed trained by the PLO. The poetry of Palestine resonated with the political mood of the times. See, for instance, the slender but significant translation of Palestinian poetry edited by M.A. Nuhman and R. Murugaiyan, *Palesteena Kavithaigal* (translated from English), VASA, Readers Association, Kalmunai, 1981.

riots, killing more than a hundred people and the destruction and loot of property of the Tamil people. Riots on this scale had not occurred since 1958.

Many militant, armed organizations,[4] including the LTTE, emerged among the Tamils during this time, most of them in and around the Jaffna peninsula, with clear leanings towards the extreme left and with a strong socialist orientation. These organizations came to capture the political imagination of the Tamil people, pushing the conventional Tamil nationalists and the Communists to the margins. In June 1981, the Jaffna Public Library, previously the American Mission Library, was burnt to ashes by certain Sinhalese miscreants with the active support of the Sri Lankan police.[5] This triggered retaliation by the Tamil armed groups against the Sri Lankan police, and led to the huge deployment of the Sri Lankan Army in the Tamil regions. This marked an end to the civilian administration of the Tamil people as we sense in the poems here of M.A. Nuhman ('Yesterday Evening, This Morning') and A. Jesurasa ('Your Plight Also').

Then in 1983, the LTTE attacked and killed thirteen soldiers of the Sri Lankan Army in Jaffna, which provoked an unprecedented all-out attack against the Tamil people all over the island. That July, when more than three thousand Tamils were killed and thousands more were forced to flee their homes (not even Tamil prisoners were spared), came to be known as Black July. Following the large-scale

[4] The Liberation Tigers of Tamil Ealam (LTTE), the People's Liberation Organization of Tamil Ealam (PLOTE), the Tamil Ealam Liberation Organization (TELO), the Ealam Revolutionary Organization of Students (EROS), the Tamil Ealam Liberation Army (TELA) and the Ealam People's Revolutionary Liberation Front (EPRLF) were some of the main organizations that were formed during this period.

[5] See the documentary *Burning Memories* directed by Sridharan Someedaran, Nihari, Chennai, 2008.

migration of the Tamil population from the Sinhalese-dominated areas into the Tamil regions in the North and the East, waves of refugees started arriving on the Tamil Nadu coast, while many other Tamils became internal refugees living in makeshift camps in various parts of Sri Lanka, and still others took refuge in a number of countries in Europe. The chain of events triggered by these riots would only reach a semblance of closure in 2009. Contemporary historians are still trying to unpack the complexities of these years.[6]

The decade following 1983 saw the issue of Sri Lankan Tamils dominating the political scene in Tamil Nadu, India, resulting in widespread protests against the Sri Lankan government and mobilization of active support for the Tamil refugees and militant Tamil organizations. The Indian government trained the militant organizations, quite in the open, often playing one against the other, even though the professed aim was to bring the Sri Lankan government to the negotiating table. Thus, Tamil Nadu, by default, became the operating base for several militant organizations. Some of them published books and magazines from Tamil Nadu, not only to promote their cause but also to bring into circulation a literature that brought together writers, ideologues and readers with a growing nascent commitment to the cause of the Tamil people beyond national borders. The Tamil public in India developed a reverence towards the Tamil militants of Sri Lanka, tracing their cultural and militant lineage from classical Tamil heroic literature. However, this did not necessarily mean a substantive engagement with Sri Lankan Tamil literature or an understanding of the

[6] Fact-finding reports for these years could be found in www.uthr.org (University Teachers for Human Rights); also in www.transcurrents.com (run by a Canada-based Sri Lankan Tamil journalist, D.B.S. Jeyaraj, accessible now, though not updated since 2012); or alternatively his current blog, www.dbsjeyaraj.com; for the LTTE-centred sources, please see www.tamilnet.com.

particular geographical and historical context of its production, even though historically there had been continuous trade and cultural contact between the two cultures. The Tamil-reading public of this period and after made possible a cultural market and this became the main source of recognition and patronage for the Sri Lankan Tamil writers. With fears of having to face separatist politics from gaining ground in its own territory, the Government of India organized several rounds of negotiations between the militants and the Sri Lankan government, even as the guerrilla warfare by the militants continued in Sri Lanka as we see here in Ranjakumar's 'Time Will Write a Song For You'.

In 1987, amidst various pacts with militant groups in Punjab and Assam, the Indian government, led by the then prime minister Rajiv Gandhi, also signed an accord with the Sri Lankan government. This pact guaranteed an amendment to the Sri Lankan Constitution, providing the Tamils with an autonomous North Eastern Administrative Region, and the withdrawal of the Sri Lankan Army from this region. The militants were supposed to lay down arms and return to the political mainstream. The period of transition was to be monitored by an Indian Peace Keeping Force (IPKF). Soon after the arrival of the IPKF in the Tamil regions—initially much to the relief of the Tamil population—the situation deteriorated drastically.[7] Unable to stop the Sri Lankan Army from harassing the Tamil people on the one hand, and unable to make the Tamil militants to surrender their arms on the other, the IPKF soon found itself cornered into an open conflict with the Tamil

[7] A particular event that precipitated the sudden change in the scenario was the fast-unto-death undertaken by the LTTE militant Dileepan, who demanded the release of Tamil militants from prisons and the end of colonization of the Tamil-speaking areas. The fast that began on 15 September 1987 lasted till 26 September 1987, when Dileepan died without succeeding in getting any of his demands.

militants, in particular with the LTTE, on behalf of the Sri Lankan state. Unfamiliar with the terrain, unequipped to deal with the urban guerrilla war tactics of the LTTE, and unable to distinguish between the people and the militants, the IPKF rapidly turned into an 'Innocent People Killing Force'[8] in the eyes of the Tamil people as seen in Tha. Agilan's story, 'A Boy's Father Dies', in this volume. Due to a curious collusion between the LTTE and the Sri Lankan government and the huge unpopularity that the IPKF gained among the public of Tamil Nadu, not to mention its own casualties, the IPKF was forced to retreat and withdraw from Sri Lanka in 1991.

After the IPKF withdrawal, the LTTE, in its effort to become the sole representative of the Tamils in Sri Lanka, embarked on a mission to eliminate all opposition, including all other Tamil militant organizations and the Tamil political leadership, with alarming ruthlessness and military discipline. It was during the same time that the LTTE decided to expel all Tamil Muslims from the Northern Province, accusing them of treachery to the Tamil cause. The Muslims were forced to leave their homes and all their belongings within two hours of the LTTE announcement. (Kumarmurthy's story, 'Hanifa and the Two Bulls', and V.I.S. Jayapalan's poem, 'The Eighth Ghost', in this volume echo this traumatic expulsion.) This eviction drove them to claim a separate

---

[8] The book *The Satanic Force*, compiled in two volumes by the LTTE in 1990–91, chronicling the atrocities committed by the IPKF in the Tamil areas, was printed in Chennai. When it was about to be published, all the printed copies were seized by the Tamil Nadu police, after the assassination of Rajiv Gandhi in 1991. However, the first volume is available in three parts as an e-book at the website: www.ebook.yarl.com, as *The Satanic Force: Heinous Crimes of Indian Peacekeeping, LTTE Headquarters, Jaffna, 1990*. For human rights violations from all sides, see Rajan Somasundaram et. al, *The Broken Palmyra: The Tamil Crisis in Sri Lanka, An Insider Account*, The Sri Lanka Studies Institute, Jaffna, 1990.

ethnic identity for themselves as Muslims who speak Tamil. All this happened when the LTTE had already resumed its war with the Sri Lankan Army (see Malaravan's 'War Journey' in this volume).

In May 1991, during his electoral campaign in Tamil Nadu, Rajiv Gandhi was assassinated by the LTTE to avenge the atrocities of the IPKF on the Tamil people. The LTTE, though, never admitted its role in this assassination. This incident put an end to the LTTE's operations in Tamil Nadu and alienated the Sri Lankan Tamil people from the Indian middle class, hitherto sympathetic to the Sri Lankan Tamil struggle. The Indian state came down heavily on any form of activity supportive of the Tamil cause, and banned the LTTE, making it difficult for even human rights-based activities to raise genuine concerns. Such measures on the part of the Indian government made it difficult for refugees from Sri Lanka to enter Tamil Nadu, not to mention the severe harassment that the refugees already living in the camps in Tamil Nadu had to face. The desperate living conditions of the Sri Lankan Tamil refugees in these camps remains largely unaddressed by all sections concerned.[9] Given this situation, the Tamils in Sri Lanka, caught between the LTTE and the Sri Lankan Army, began their perilous journeys seeking asylum in Europe, Canada and Australia, thus marking the beginning of a new Tamil Diaspora. By 1995, the Sri Lankan Army was able to chase the LTTE out of Jaffna, sparking another spate of internal migration of the Tamil people from the Jaffna region into Vanni and vice versa, as reflected in Nilanthan's poem 'Earthen Towns'. Confined to the Vanni region and the East, the LTTE gradually transformed itself from a guerrilla force into a conventional army,

[9] Hardly any account exists of the plight of the Sri Lankan refugees in India. One exception is Tho. Pathinathan's *Porin Marupakkam, Eala Agathiyin Thuyara Varalaru*, Kalachuvadu, Nagerkovil, 2007. Also, Mullai Jesudasan's *Neelam Aagi Varum Kadal*, Nidarsanam, Tamil Ealam, 2003.

running a parallel administration, with Killinocchi as the capital of their de facto state. The Vanni region remained entirely cut off from the rest of the world, placed as it was under an economic embargo by the Sri Lankan state from 1995 to 2002. The LTTE consolidated itself during this period, within Vanni as well as among the Diaspora, strengthening its international networks of finance, weapons, and culture. It consciously built a heroic image for itself as the saviour of the Tamil people, very much modelled on the popular cultural means adopted by the Dravidian political parties in Tamil Nadu. It's a different story that it was never able to distance itself from its reputation as a terrorist outfit.

After 11 September 2001, in a changed global scenario, a ceasefire agreement was reached between the LTTE and the Sri Lankan government, mediated by Norway on behalf of the international community and covertly supported by India. The peace lasted from 2002 to 2004, making it possible for people living in the Vanni region to see the world and for the world to see the ravages of war. By 2005, the ceasefire was violated on both sides several times and war was once again imminent. Mahinda Rajapaksa was elected President, probably helped by the abstention from the electoral process forced on the Tamil people by the LTTE. In 2006, the Sri Lankan Army launched an all-out, no-holds-barred war on the LTTE and the people in the Vanni region, boxing them from all sides. Several thousands of people were killed in the continuous aerial bombardments and ground-based missile attacks, and the survivors were forced to flee from place to place, ending up on the Mullaittivu coast, as we see in Nilanthan's epic poem 'Yugapuranam' in this volume. In this war without respite, thousands of Tamil people hoped in vain for help from India or the USA. In May 2009, the Sri Lankan government proclaimed victory over the LTTE, and announced the death of the LTTE chief V. Prabhakaran.

The reasons cited for the tragic collapse of the LTTE in 2009 are various: the weariness of the war-afflicted people of Vanni, who had gone through two decades of war, with almost every family forced to send at least one member to war and most certainly losing them (Deebachelvan's poem 'Let's Move on Again, to Yet Another Place' has echoes of this trauma); the changed world order that choked off arms supply to the LTTE; an altered global political landscape which seemed to have exhausted any sympathy for movements fighting for self-determination anywhere in the world; the implosion of the LTTE's carefully constructed myth about itself as a supreme heroic force; and the failure of any international forum to come to the rescue of the war-ravaged Tamil population, even when it verged on genocide, compounded by the Tamil Diaspora's inability to mobilize any semblance of international pressure on the Sri Lankan state.

The end of the war has not brought any respite for the surviving Tamil population in the Vanni region. Even after five years, they continue to live in makeshift camps under the constant surveillance of the army; there has been absolute refusal to account for the thousands who went missing during the war. Tamils in other regions of Sri Lanka live in a forced peace under a symbolically elected provincial administration bereft of any real power. There are clear signs that the Sri Lankan government will execute its plan to resettle the Tamil regions with the Sinhalese people. The Tamil Muslim population, still without any means to return to their homes, are being targeted once again, this time, again by the Sinhalese majority. The working masses on the plantations, equally ravaged by the war, are yet to find a space for themselves.[10] The Sri Lankan media is constantly under a very real threat of abductions and killings.

[10] See the recent report by Meera Srinivasan, 'Elections hold little hope for "plantation Tamils"', in *The Hindu*, Chennai, 20 September 2014, p. 12.

The Tamil Diaspora without a centre to hold them together is reconciling itself to the impossibility of a Tamil homeland, notwithstanding the simulations of victimhood and glory projected by Dravidian sentiments soaked in Tamil nationalism. Another phenomenon on the rise is the growth of a Hindu fundamentalism with aspirations of being part of a subcontinental Hindu majority, consciously orchestrated by right-wing groups trying to destroy the distinct Sri Lankan Tamil identity, and with aims to subsume even the whole of Sri Lanka within its inherently imperialist project. In such a fragmented context, there are only islands of despair, perhaps looking to literature for hope.

People, Struggle and Their Literature

Tamil in India and in Sri Lanka was shaped by a common literary heritage. This is evident in the works of Arumuga Navalar (1822–1879) and C.W. Damodara Pillai (1832–1901) in nineteenth-century Jaffna, who reinvented the classical Tamil corpus in print. Despite this common heritage, Sri Lankan Tamil differs widely from Indian Tamil due to a number of factors. The island's distinct material culture and landscape (Jaffna has no rivers, for instance!) has produced unique dialects. Portuguese and Dutch colonial rule played a part in the codification of caste rules. The American Mission made substantial contributions in the fields of education and translation (the Jaffna Public Library's collection of manuscripts and books was testimony to this, before it was burnt down in 1981).[11] The Mission and the Saivite response to it helped constitute a unique system of education in Tamil up to the level of the University which insulated their Tamil from the ever-pervasive

[11] S. Jebansesan, *The American Mission and Modern Education in Jaffna: The Contribution of Higher Educational Enterprise of the American Missionaries in Nineteenth Century*, Kumaran Book House, Colombo–Chennai, 2013.

influence of English. This helped Sri Lankan Tamil, in both its written and spoken forms, to retain a classical flavour, a source of pride for its speakers.

Despite its distinct character, Sri Lankan Tamil literature since the early twentieth century has remained under the shadow of its big brother, Indian Tamil literature. Due to the skewed nature of the market, Sri Lankan Tamil literature was not widely available to the Tamil-reading public in India, whereas the Sri Lankan market was flooded with Indian Tamil popular literature and cinema. As in India, Tamil literature in early twentieth-century Sri Lanka was divided into popular magazines of large circulation and small journals. The history of modern Sri Lankan Tamil literature, in fact, is conventionally divided into periods marked by the publication of important journals, such as the *Eala Kesari* phase (1930–1958), the *Marumalarcchi* phase (1946–1948) and the *Dinakaran* phase (1932–). Literature of this early period was primarily reformist in orientation, inclined towards social criticism and romance, and written in a highly formal prose full of authorial commentary.

Two distinct literary trends dominated the period between 1956 and the 1970s: progressive literature (*murpokku ilakkiyam*), modelled on social realism; and another body of literature supposedly loyal to art and aesthetics. The progressive literature movement was spearheaded by two Marxist scholars, K. Kailasapathi[12] (1933–1982) and K. Sivathambi[13] (1932–2011), trained in England by the

[12] Professor K. Kailasapathi was a literary historian, critic and journalist from Jaffna, and is well known for his Marxist analysis of classical Sangam Tamil literature. (K. Kailasapathi, *Tamil Heroic Poetry*, Clarendon Press, Oxford, 1968.) He was also the editor of the *Dinakaran* daily, from 1958–1962.

[13] K. Sivathambi, professor of literature and a critic, was from Jaffna, and is known for his work, *Drama in Ancient Tamil Society* (New Century Book House, Chennai, 1981).

British Marxist scholar George Thomson.[14] The activities of the Communist party and the Progressive Writers' Association in this period inspired many young writers of the working class. Their writings altered the middle-class ethos which had defined literary production until then. Grounding themselves in the realities of the Sri Lankan Tamil rural landscape and its caste hierarchy, they brought dialects into literature (See Dominic Jeeva in this volume). Importantly, writers from the plantations were brought into the Tamil literary mainstream by this movement.[15] The other trend did not have a defined leadership, though Mu. Thalaiyasingam provided a critique of the dominant social realist literature and emphasized the self and aesthetics over material relations. By the beginning of the 1970s, in the context of the increased oppression by the Sri Lankan state in the Tamil-speaking regions, a neorealist literature was in the making, in which the author turned into a mute observer. The journal *Alai* (1975–1984, a total of thirty-five issues), then published from Jaffna, is representative of this kind of writing.

After Black July, with the publication of the poetry anthology *Maranathul Vaazhvom*[16] (To Live in Death), the war literature of Sri Lankan Tamil was born. The violence of the army and the guerrilla attacks of the militants, along with a stark fear of living preoccupied the literary imagination. This period also witnessed the beginning of various militant organizations starting their own publications

---

[14] A discussion about the role of pioneering Tamil scholars like Xavier Thaninayagam (1913–1980) and Su. Vithiyanandan (1924–1989) in the Sri Lankan Tamil struggle is beyond the scope of this Introduction.

[15] To name a few writers of this movement: Se. Yoganathan (1941–2008), Dominic Jeeva (1927–), Ganesalingan (1927–), Thelivathai Joesph (1934–) and Anthony Jeeva (1944–). The last two are from the upcountry region.

[16] Cheran, Yesurasa et.al, *Maranathul Vaazhvom*, 1996, Vitiyal, Coimbatore. First edition 1986, Jaffna.

and journals, which involved translations of poetry and political theory from English, along with the creative process of producing a literature of advocacy and propaganda,[17] not to mention certain dissident writings[18] from within these organizations. Much of this was facilitated by the movement of writers and militants between Tamil Nadu and Sri Lanka. Later in 1990, with the expulsion of Tamil Muslims from the Northern Province by the LTTE, there was the emergence of a Tamil Muslim literature, differentiating itself from the rest, and seeking an identity for itself. After the LTTE retreated into the Vanni region, and established their de facto state, they formed their own publication department and produced 'official' propaganda literature and also translations of technical (medical, engineering, law, warfare) literature from all over the world into Tamil. They also published their own literary journals, providing a platform for writers from Vanni. Some writers living in Vanni also self-published their writings during this period. These publications were largely unknown to the world, with their circulation limited to Vanni and a section of the Diaspora. Unfortunately, none of this survived the final war in 2009, with the Archives and the Library of the LTTE wiped out.

The late 1990s witnessed the arrival of the Tamil Diaspora based in Europe, Canada and Australia, into the world of literature. Through their publications, journals, theatre and cinema, they were able to express in Tamil their newfound anxieties in different landscapes (for the first time in the history of Tamil literature, there was 'snow') and their experiences of a newly felt freedom (see Ki. Pi. Aravinthan and Aruntati in

[17] For example, see Arular, *Lanka Rani*, 2008 (1980, first edition), Saanron Pathippagam, London and Chennai.

[18] Govindan, *Puthiyathor Ulagam*, Theeppori, 1985, place of publication not known.

this volume), providing contemporary Tamil a place in the civil society and universities of the western world. The publication of literary anthologies from London, Paris and Toronto, which brought together writings from Sri Lanka and from the Diaspora, provided a much-needed avenue for these writers. But along with their deeply felt nostalgia for Tamil, the Diaspora also retained their religious culture and caste system. Mired in the polarized politics of pro- and anti-LTTE, they managed to sustain a vibrant cultural activism in foreign lands. By the end of the 1990s, the Sri Lankan Diaspora also turned into a market for the Indian Tamil publishing world, which used it to commercial advantage. For the Tamil middle class in India, Sri Lankan Tamil remained exotic, familial, but not intimate (there is not a single Sri Lankan Tamil restaurant of any kind, in the whole of Tamil Nadu!). The Diasporic literary world, on the other hand, started to gravitate towards the Indian Tamil literary world, mimicking current fads in Indian Tamil and anticipating recognition from it, but oblivious to the instrumentalities of the Indian Tamil publishing and literary networks. On the other hand, the Diaspora did not consciously engage with the literary traditions of their new homes either. This may change in the near future, with the next generation of the Diaspora increasingly turning to the languages of their adopted nations to express themselves, and producing a Sri Lankan Tamil literature in English or in French. It is very difficult to discuss in concrete terms the nature of circulation and reading practices of Sri Lankan Tamil literature, as no institutional spaces exist for it—not even a bookshop or a library.[19] The traffic of printed material between India, Sri Lanka and other countries of the Tamil

---

[19] A joint effort of concerned individuals based in Colombo, and supported by the Tamil Diaspora maintains a website, www.noolaham.net as a digital platform for Sri Lankan Tamil literature.

Diaspora continues in haphazard, unpredictable ways, making access to this literature difficult.[20]

Now we have before us a Sri Lankan Tamil literature which has branched into several micro-literatures from different regions in Sri Lanka: Dalit literature, Muslim literature, hill-country literature, war literature, popular literature, feminist literature, Diaspora literature, and so on.

Time Will Write a Song for You

This anthology is an outcome of the research programme of Contemporary Tamil Culture at the French Institute of Pondicherry, which tries to collect, organize, preserve and study the sources of contemporary Tamil literature.[21] The anthology has been translated and edited by four researchers affiliated to the French Institute of Pondicherry, none of Sri Lankan Tamil origin. The works included in this anthology have not been selected for the context or the situation in which they were written. They themselves are the context, for the simple reason that when read only for their context, or outside of their context, they are susceptible to voyeurism. We have chosen works which are singular and universal in their expression, which can stand alongside anything in the world republic of letters—such as the works of Juan Gelman, cited at the beginning of this Introduction, or Kafka, cited at the end. A major portion of this anthology is comprised of poetry, which remains without doubt the high point of achievement in Sri Lankan Tamil literature. Even in its free-verse

[20] It is puzzling to note that through all these years of turmoil, with people facing oppression from the Sri Lankan state, their literature never faced active censorship from it, except for curbs on distribution between regions, during different periods.

[21] The Research Programme and the Library at the French Institute of Pondicherry has the single largest collection in India of Sri Lankan Tamil journals, magazines, books and documentaries.

form, this poetry, quite distinct from Indian Tamil poetry, sustains an element of lyricism derived from classical prosody, yet grounded in the registers of folk and spoken Tamil. (See the poems of Mahakavi, Neelavanan and Mu. Ponnampalam.) It is a poetry which can be sung and staged. It is not a coincidence that many Sri Lankan Tamil poets until the 1980s were also exemplary performers of their own and others' poetry, such as Vilvarathinam, V.I.S. Jayapalan, Cheran and Nilanthan. However, this performative lyricism often lent itself to moments of simple escapism and euphoria, away from reality rather than returning to it. The poetry of the 1990s' generation breaks away from this lyricism, probably due to the stark reality of the war that surrounded them (see, for example, the poems by Sivaramani, Vinodhine, Faheema Jahan, Bose Nilhale, Majeed, Deebachelvan and others) and the emergent influence of Indian Tamil poetry, which lost its lyrical quality a long time ago.

We have not been able to include the works of the Communist Dalit writer K. Daniel[22] (1927–1986) because they are predominantly novels, infused with dialects to which a mere excerpt will not do any justice. We have not included plays despite their significant role in the social life of Sri Lankan Tamils, most importantly in the reformist struggles against untouchability and during the later stages of the militant struggle.[23] These are strong texts

---

[22] K. Daniel, who belonged to a family of *vannar* (launderers), was a political activist of the Maoist faction of the Communist party, known for his role in the 'Popular Movement for the Eradication of Untouchability'. *Pancamar (1972)* remains his most important novel, but a series of five others complete a faithful picture of the struggle of the untouchables in Sri Lankan Tamil society. He is often considered the pioneer of Dalit literature in Tamil.

[23] A staged play that had a very important role in the anti-caste struggle is *Kandan Karunai*, written by N.K. Raghunathan in 1968, and staged by many directors. See N.K. Raghunathan, *Kandan Karunai*, Desiya Kalai Ilakkiya Peravai, Colombo, 2003.

of performance, embedded in folk music and theatre, but may not reverberate in translation.[24] We have also omitted populist, sensational writings aimed at the Indian Tamil world which made the Sri Lankan Tamil world exotic. Certain iconic representatives of Sri Lankan Tamil literature do not figure in our collection, as they are already available in translation. However, we really regret our inability to include more works from upcountry Tamils, whose politics and continuing conditions of oppression have stifled their literary endeavours to realism and mobilizational idioms.[25] One might be surprised to find the name of Piramil (1939–1997) in this anthology as he is well known in Tamil Nadu, where he spent the major part of his life. However, he remained a Sri Lankan Tamil in letter and spirit as well as in his unique understanding of the crisis on the island as a 'collective suicide' of a nation.[26]

The works collected here force us to think about unthinkable experiences of violence, displacement, dispossession and vulnerability. These experiences seem in stark contrast to our relatively comfortable lives, and at the same time, the writing brings

---

[24] An important playwright of this period is Kulandai M. Shanmugalingam, whose plays are available in English. See S. Pathmanathan (Sopa) (trans.), *Shamugalingam Three Plays*, Kumaran Book House, Colombo and Chennai, 2007.

[25] The most well known of the upcountry writers are Thelivathai Joseph and Anthony Jeeva. The journal *Theerthakarai* (1980–1982), which had five issues, provided a platform for a new generation of upcountry Tamil writers. See Nandalala (ed.), *Theerthakarai Kathaigal (Ilangai Malaiyaga Sirukathaigal)*, Annam, Sivagangai, 1995. Also the anthology edited by Manimekalai Kamalakanthan, *Malaiyaga Parisuk Kathaigal*, Kalai Oli Muthaiya Pillai Ninaivu Kuzhu, Colombo, 1994.

[26] See his book *Piramil Dharmod Jeevaramu, Srilankavin Desiya Tharkolai*, Parivartana Publishers, Chennai, 1984. Not many are aware that he translated books for Tamil militants and even wrote a national anthem for Tamil Ealam. See Piramil, *Pirmail Kavithaigal*, Layam, Sathiyamangalam, 1998, p. 223.

them uncomfortably close, making us unsure whether to identify with the human in them or recoil at the inhuman—reminding us, perhaps, that what we call inhumanity is all too human. But this literature is not simply of interest as a reflection of or response to civil war and ethnic violence. It is incisive, analytical, abstract, detailed, dreamlike, lyrical, satirical, allusive, layered and multi-vocal. The writers represented in this collection are both individually and stylistically diverse. They hail from different regions and religions, and their writing ranges from the powerfully simple to the highly experimental. This anthology presents a literature that expresses hope and life amidst oppression, violence and death, with lucidity and rigour, a literature which is under grave threat of being silenced by the prevailing politics in the region. At this point the sirens are still singing, what is to be feared is their silence.[27]

On Translation

The translation of Sri Lankan writing from Tamil presents some particular difficulties. The left-branching syntax of Tamil makes the order of images, so important in poetry and even in prose, difficult to replicate in English; we have gone case-by-case in determining whether it is possible to retain the order of images without compromising rhythm and the minimum of clarity. In experimental writing such as Gowribalan's, it is sometimes difficult at first even to sort out the referents of a long sentence. The internal diversity of Tamil as represented in the texts—its distinct 'written' and 'spoken' varieties, and the dialect spoken in Sri Lanka—and its interaction with Sinhalese present more problems. In this anthology, Sinhalese words have been footnoted. As 'spoken' Tamil appears mainly in the dialogues of the short stories, it has been rendered by all the

---

[27] Franz Kafka, 'The Silence of the Sirens', in Nahum N. Glatzer (ed.), Franz Kafka, *The Complete Stories*, Schocken Books, New York, 1971, pp. 430–432.

translators in more or less colloquial English. The particularities of Sri Lankan Tamil that may appear in the stories or the poems have gone unremarked, as the markers of dialect are often subtle differences in word choice, usage and pronunciation which are not easy to represent even in the standardized language, much less in another language altogether.

Translations for this anthology were done by two native speakers of Tamil and two non-native Tamil speakers, with active inputs from the authors themselves, particularly in the case of Vilvarathinam and Gowribalan. Hence, to us, the process of translation was a delicate negotiation with varied sensibilities, but with a unified conviction that a translation is not an explanation. We feel that translation is an act of learning, of reading, and of writing, as a powerful piece of writing makes us want to write it again in a new language. We say this 'not with complacency, but feeling our shortcomings in every bone'.[28]

Kannan M.
Rebecca Whittington
D. Senthil Babu
David C. Buck

[28] Jibanananda Das, *Malloban*, 1948.

The Temple Car and the Moon

Mahakavi

'the whole town together is pulling a temple car,
come, let's take hold of the rope,'
someone came and said.

he too was a son born
to the worldmother, borne
in her suffering womb to live here for a hundred years.
one with broad shoulders
and big arms, with light in his eyes, with a heart that would like to
be delivered from worry;

he came; he was a young man;
a human.
a younger brother of the one who, the day before,
fluttering his wings of thought, had climbed into the sky
touched the full moon and returned
a very hard-working man!

'in this world we should all stand together
in harmony.' saying this with a sweet ardour,
he came to bow his head in prayer and take the rope.

'stand still!' said one man.
'stop!' said another.
'shit!' said one.
'scum!' said yet another.

'speak!' said one.
'burn!' said a different one.

a stone fell
a neck cut
lips split against teeth
red water streaming out
reddening the earth
there was a struggle
and a man killed.
the temple car the whole town was to pull together
jerked to a halt as if it had grown roots
the mother who once produced the whole world
sat down dumbstruck at the sight
of her own offspring's frenzy.

look, there rolls in dirt
kith and kin of the one
who touched the full moon
just the day before!

Translated by Rebecca Whittington

Mahakavi, *Therum Thingalum* (early 1960s), in M.A. Nuhman and Jesurasa (eds), *Patinoru Eelattu Kavingargal*, CreA, Chennai, 1984, pp. 27–28

Enlightenment

Dominic Jeeva

Jaffna. Third Cross Street. A corner nuzzling the warehouse street. To its west, the Poun* Mark warehouse. About ten yards from the warehouse—like an impassioned, restless young woman—stood a municipal street light, in solitude. Perched on its top, the flickering bulb, like a lantern lit by fireflies, its feeble rays striking a faint light on the ground. Tramping on his own shadow, with one hand supporting the lamp post, shaking his head like a lizard, stood Big Brother 'Shokolo' ('how wonderful') Kandaiah.

One can easily tell that he is in his state of Enlightenment. Siddhartha experienced Enlightenment on a full moon day during the month of Vaishaki, but Kandaiah attains his Enlightenment at times like this. Since it is now palm toddy season it's easy to get a share of toddy and a cigar for a mere 20 catam. Kandaiah never misses this opportunity. After nine, he surrenders himself to the power of the fermented intoxicant and attains his enlightened state.

Today, now, it's nine.

Enlightenment has been born in Big Brother Kandaiah.

Big brother Kandaiah is a loner with no home, no family ties. Hefting loads of roofing tiles in the Poun Mark warehouse is his occupation. Just south of the warehouse, in the all-expansive ocean, cargo boats from Kallikkottai lie at anchor in Aluppandi harbour. Some twenty men and women lug tiles on their heads from these boats to the warehouse. They carry their tile loads all day long, and collect their two-rupee wage each evening.

* A *poun* is a measure used in weighing gold, equivalent to eight grams.

Among the workers forced to run a 'pinch-belly family' on that measly income, Kandaiah the Loner is a prince, alright. The other workers all call him Big Brother Kandaiah—it doesn't matter if they are actually younger or older than he is. Because he often says 'shokolo' when he talks, that honorific title gets stuck to his name as well.

In his non-enlightened state, Kandaiah is a good man for sure. During those hours, he is pretty jovial with his colleagues Adaikkalamuthu, Rafael, Mary Pillai and Lourdamma. True enough, he usually keeps his distance from them, but there are moments when he gets really friendly.

Sometimes they all sit under the shade of the tree in front of the warehouse, drinking black tea brought in old fabric-bleach tins from a nearby tea shop; they chew their betel leaves, talk loud, and laugh a lot. Even though Kandaiah won't drink tea with the rest of the workers, he is particular about not missing those sessions. And when he tosses his discoloured red head-rest towel over his shoulders and joins in, there is no end to fun. When Lourdamma is also there, the banter gets really spicy. Folk songs and dances are staged with fine music.

Lourdamma twists up her betel-coloured lips and baits him, 'What's up, Big Brother Kandaiah? You're strutting around, acting silly like a bridegroom today!'

'Oh yes . . . yes . . . you're looking to get me to put a ring on your finger and marry you, ain't ya? That's what you want, isn't it? Hmm . . . Shokolo . . . here, gimme a pinch of tobacco,' he says.

'Ha . . . There's nothing wrong with borrowing a little tobacco . . . but just look at you, always borrowing tobacco like a besotted husband,' Lourdamma says, handing him a bit of tobacco from the little box hanging off her waist.

'How come Big Brother Kandaiah keeps getting his tobacco just from Lourdamma? Is there something going on here? I wonder what's at stake?' teases Mary Pillai, fiddling with her coarse, greying hair above her forehead.

'What about her? She is not a grandma like you . . . she's young . . . she's just a girl,' Kandaiah says.

These are hardly matters of love. Lourdamma is the youngest of the lot and happens to be pretty, but only in comparison to the rest of the women—like an *iluppai* flower when you have no sugar. Everybody gets a kick out of making her the butt of their jokes. When Kandaiah participates in these 'games', he acts like he's just the equal of the other people who work there—the tile carriers from the *cheri*. However, when he forgets himself in a trance, Kandaiah never forgets his pride in his own caste.

But to articulate that he has to reach his enlightened state. Once he gets there, his song begins: 'Shokolo . . . Who do you take me for? Lifting tiles does not make me a Pariah . . . I am a Vellala, man, a Vellala of the Cankiliar lineage, who once ruled Nallur! I am not of a low caste . . . not of a rising caste, man . . . Hmmm . . . Shokolo . . . My caste is Shokolo Supreme.'

The next morning, when he wakes up, he is the same old tile-hefting Kandaiah. Then, to him, Adaikkalamuthu is still Adaikkalamuthu, Rafael is still Rafael, Mary Pillai is still Mary Pillai, and Lourdamma is still Lourdamma.

But, for the moment, the Kandaiah standing with the support of the street light is well into his state of Enlightenment!

Yesterday too, he arrived in this same state of Enlightenment. He held forth at the same spot and proclaimed his artful wisdom to the world. That time the clerk pulled him up and said, "What's going on, Kandaiah? I hear you get yourself drunk every night and disturb the neighbourhood?' Kandaiah could not take that, and he drank with a vengeance.

Here he was, in his state of revelation, standing under the same lamp post, just looking around. In front of him was that thatched hut. Third Cross Street is where respectable, civilized people live. Just this one thatched hut stands in isolation like a curry leaf tree sapling, an eyesore. Adaikkalamuthu and his family live in it. He hefts tiles like everybody else, but somehow he earned a 'good boy' reputation from the warehouse managers, and got the nightwatchman's post as well. He was proud of his watchman's position, which earned him this thatched hut, without rent.

Enlightened Kandaiah's nightly habit was to stand under his favourite lamp post, next to this hut, and offer 'worship' through his enchanting songs of Enlightenment. Setting himself up to drink his palm toddy, he suspected that this Adaikkalamuthu might be the one who told the clerk about him. Then, through his blessed service to the Lord of the Toddy, that suspicion rooted in him as a certain truth.

'I know—I know for sure who grumbled to Mister Clerk about me being a drunkard. Shokolo . . . So, I drink. Hey man—Adaikkalamuthu! Do I take money out of your father's house to get drunk? Even if I do carry tiles around, I am a Vellala—damn it—of the great Cankiliar's legacy. You are a Pariah, the lowest of the low castes, man. You showed off your low-caste mentality there. Swear to God, I do drink. What's it to you, damn you? Shokolo . . . You son of a Pariah, come on outside. I'll show you—I'll smash all your joints.' He stood there and hurled these challenges at Adaikkalamuthu.

'Hey, Big Brother Kandaiah! It's dark and people are going to sleep. Go on home and eat, and go to bed.'

'Shaat-aaap-yur-movuth in the white man's language means shut your mouth tight. Am I the son of a damn Pariah like you? I am a single man, I'm on my own. I toss some money out, Shokolo, and there's my food. I sleep where I choose, on anyone's porch . . . but you, man, you have gone and shown the mentality of your caste. Let me take care of you first, get arrested and stuff myself up with food there.'

Adaikkalamuthu decided not to prolong the rant. He shut his gate.

'I am the King of the Cankilis, celebrated in all three worlds,' continued Kandaiah's rhymes. He acted them out in street-drama style, interspersed with the choicest of swear words that substituted for the absent drumbeats.

'Who's that, man?'

That was not Adaikkalamuthu's voice, Kandaiah realized despite his spiritual trance.

He looked deeper.

Two policemen on patrol down the street.

'Who's there? What's all this dancing in the street? You must be Kandaiah. We've received a lot of "complaints" about you. People around here are losing sleep because of you. What do you think you're doing, boy, abusing people like this? Does your body require some "attention"? Do you want our special "camel treatment"?' threatened one of the policemen.

'Who? Me? Abusing? Oh god! No way! Don't I know that my tongue will rot in hell if I swear at people? Where did you get this devil's tale from?'

'That's as may be, boy, but this is the last time. If there are any more complaints about you getting drunk and prancing around in the streets, that's it.'

'I swear on Muniyappan of the fort. Why would I drink? Why would I shout?' Kandaiah melted, squirmed, twisted, drooled, begged and somehow managed to get rid of the policemen yesterday.

However, today's flourish is way more than yesterday's.

With his arm extending to the municipal lamp post for support, Brother Shokolo Kandaiah vividly remembered what the policemen said yesterday. And it hurt. His suspicion, that Adaikkalamuthu must be behind their annoyance, assumed gigantic proportions.

He started shouting, determined that his voice should pierce right through the sleeping little hut.

'Shokolo . . . Hey Adaikkalamuthu! You low-caste son of a Pariah! Was it you that told on me to the police, damn you? . . . That measly policeman that came around yesterday actually cursed me . . . He threatened to chew me up if I did any more prancing around in the street, didn't he? I would have smashed them both into little pieces, but I took pity on them and let them go. Who am I? Lifting tiles does not make me a son of a Pariah. I belong to the glorious lineage of the Cankiliars, man! Shokolo . . . Hey Adaikkalamuthu! . . . Bring on your policemen now. I'll take care of them with one hand,' Kandaiah screams.

As if destined to appear, the same two policemen are heading this way.

'What's up, Kandaiah? Your body feels "sour"? Needs some real treatment, huh?'

Come what may, I shall never flinch in front of these policemen again, swore Kandaiah to himself, and he took a swig of the toddy. So, unmindful of the consequences, he starts talking.

'Do you know who I am, Policeman, sir? I belong to the valiant and glorious lineage of the Cankiliars. I am not a Pariah,' says Kandaiah, squirming again.

The khaki shirts cannot tolerate that insult. Their rage rises up all the way, out of their noses, they leap on Kandaiah and maul him . . .

Kandiah lies there, whimpering . . .

The two policemen disappear, leaving no trace that they had ever come. They talk about upholding the law, but they seem to have mastered the art of breaking it . . .

Everybody living in that street was well aware of the thrashing received by Kandaiah. But all the elites' doorways were shut tight.

Silence. Ripping right through it, a recurring groan . . .

'Who am I? An orphan with nobody . . . An orphan without

a single soul to question this injustice . . . Who is here for me?' Shokolo Big Brother Kandaiah muttered into his own mouth, in agony.

Fearfully, fearfully, with a hurricane lantern in his hand, bringing his son along, Adaikkalamuthu comes out to look at Kandaiah.

Severe beating. Blood gushing from the head. Splashing some water on the wound and organizing first aid, Adaikkalamuthu asks his son to get a taxi.

The taxi arrives.

Adaikkalamuthu and his son together help Kandaiah into the car. Kandaiah regains a bit of his consciousness . . .

The taxi rushes to the hospital.

Still intoxicated and wavering in the realm of Enlightenment, Kandaiah's mouth rambles on and on.

'Hey, do you know who I am? Did you policemen fall from the sky, huh? . . . Adaikkalamuthu, you low-caste Pariah scum. Watch out! I might carry roof tiles, but I am not a Pariah, damn it . . . I belong to the lineage of the great King Cankili, man! The dual heritage, purebred Vellala lineage, damn it . . .'

Translated by D. Senthil Babu

Dominic Jeeva, *'Gnanam'* (around early 1960s), in *Dominic Jeeva Sirukataikal*, Mallikaippantal, Jaffna, 1996, pp. 109–118

To His Holiness Arumuga Navalar*: An Appeal

Mu. Thalaiyasingam

Dear Father, Greetings:

It's a hundred or so years since you passed away, and I am a son in this Tamil lineage that is finally organizing a memorial celebration for you. I don't know what you would make of our leaders organizing this sort of a festival such a long time after the fact, but to me it is a big deal. Just think: now, delayed by a hundred years, we really are putting this grand festival together. As far as our Tamil people are concerned, we can truthfully call this a huge achievement.

The situation in today's Jaffna—oh, now that is an altogether different story, Father, far worse than those old stories that you saw with your own eyes! Your passions and your goals are coming to fruition here and now, but totally upside down. It's true that there is a rush of devotees jostling for a place in the line at temples on every street corner, and it's true that spectacles of gods and goddesses appear on wall posters everywhere—but people these days just pay a bit of money to see things you tried to see in your searching, your singing, and your wanderings. They see it in songs and in screenplays. They dissect their viewings of it into 'First Class', 'Second Class', and 'Gallery', then stand on tiptoe while they

* Arumuga Navalar (1822–1879) was a very influential Hindu—specifically Saivite—revivalist Tamil scholar, popularly celebrated as the Father of Tamil prose; a reformer in the academic sense with missionary influence but a casteist to the core. The dominant Vellala Saivite society in Jaffna has a tradition of deifying him.

worship it. (You must excuse me if these words no longer carry meanings that are familiar to you.)

Festivals in the morning, festivals in the middle of the day, festivals in the evening, festivals at night! Sometimes these spectacles even take place after midnight. You could never have imagined these temples! But that does not mean things are any better now than what you must have witnessed in your day and time. We have all these dramas: 'lockouts', 'picket lines', 'satyagraha', 'police security', 'confrontation', 'fights', and so on. Mostly—please note the emphasis on 'mostly'—these are the popular temples and festivals of today, our gods and our goddesses! It's not that we are bereft of leaders: during election times one of them sprouts up on every corner. Then there is education, all the way up to university. But all these different sorts of pompous robots manufactured by the University focus only on employability, to the point that they forget all about Tamil, about religion and about freedom. Father, this is the situation these days in Jaffna. It seems awful, does it not? Now tell me: in this state of affairs, is it not a huge achievement to stage a festival that neither ignores you, nor Tamil nor religion?

If you were here today, what would you do, Father? Actually, that is not my most important question, but I'll ask it anyway. Please, though, whatever you say, just don't tell me I have to write another castigation. After all, aren't all of these dramas taking place well after you wrote your own blistering castigations? What we need is something else. Dreams take form when you castigate and push things down—not just in an individual, but that's what happens in the wider society as well. When you hold things down, then push down on yet more things—even when those things suffocate more and more, even when their horizons are more and more restricted—what is suppressed will burst forth as factions, and as dreams. They set up sheds on every street corner and decorate them with wall posters. They wait in line. But what do they see in all these things if not just dreams? A collective dream! Will all your condemnations and mass meetings eradicate these things? I do not think so, Father. On the contrary it seems to me that they might even be functioning as long-distance aids in causing them.

I do not like your castigations. Now, do not think that this generation intimidates me, for after all, I am one of them. No, I am not scared. It's just that, as inadequate as their dreams and their factions are, your own critiques also seem to me incomplete, on an aimless terrain. What we need is a new path. Love, love! There—those dream-lovers whistling and clowning around inside their sheds: would you find it in yourself to embrace them, too? And those faction-lovers roaming from street to street, carrying their placards and shouting their slogans: would you accept them too? I mean, would you want to embrace and guide them too? Could you do that? Would you even consider doing that? Well, in any case whatever your reactions, to us it seems that this is not only possible, but particularly important. In fact, it is the first thing we want to do. People who have been marginalized, crushed and exploited are not embraced and included and nurtured in our religion and in our tradition; so this tradition and this religion do not strike us as worthy of our praise, nor of our support, Father. Actually, the Tamil and the Saivism that you fostered only crushes them and pushes them even farther to the margins. It crushes them, and it crushes them, and it causes them to dream. It makes them scream. You never realized it, but all your critiques were hurled against people who were just holding out a helping hand to them. Maybe in your day you thought it necessary to castigate people who stepped up to hold out a helping hand when you yourself would not lift a finger. Now, however, Father, we see through all that. So today we are asking for a different path. Love, love! Are you capable of showing that now?

I don't know if our situation and our needs would make much sense to you. We would like to explain them to you, patiently.

Father, I must admit something right at the outset. As thoughts about you have grown inside me, I have come to realize that I feel an immeasurable sense of connection to you. Everything I read about you and about your service to Tamil and to religion captivates me. I get restless, and I pace back and forth. It astonishes me how you were able to utilize whatever you needed to fulfil your objectives in those days. The printing press, magazines, schools, the publishing of books, prayers, sermons—they all flourished when touched by your hands. Why, even your condemnations served your ends extremely well. I do not deny that.

But your objectives were limited to Saivism and to Tamil, where they stopped. They never went beyond that to touch and reform the foundations of society. Enraged as you were by the proselytizing efforts of other religions, you failed to see the gangrenous cruelties of caste, and the narrow-mindedness that lies embedded in our own society, and which handed victory to those very proselytizers. Vallalar of Vadalur* saw them right away. Not only did he see the dictatorship and the exploitation that went in the name of caste, but he also saw the rule of arrogance and the war cry of ignorance that went in the name of religion. Maybe it was the India he lived in that showed that to him. That is why he tried to develop and act upon visions that future worlds would find astonishing, and revere him for. But the times were not yet ripe for his plans to mature,

---

* Navalar vehemently denounced Vallalar as a religious impostor. See, for example, *Poliyarutpaa Maruppu* in *Piripanta-t-Tirattu*, pages 89–121. Vallalar's real name was Chidambaram Ramalingam (1823–1874). He was a Saiva saint and a poet. Within the Saiva sect, he was a radical who dared to address issues of inequality and poverty. He was the founder of the humanist movement Samarasa Sutha Sanmarkka Sangam. His followers believe that he disappeared into the light of the '*aruljothi*', which he worshipped. For the dispute between Vallalar and Navalar, please see P. Saravanan, *Arutpa Marutpa Kandanathirattu*, Kalachuvadu, Nagerkovil, 2010.

nor did he try hard enough to nurture them. Fundamentally, he was an itinerant philosopher, going wherever his mind and his god (Siva) led him. I do not think he tried very hard to subject his wisdom to the power of knowledge and action. So, because his disciples were bereft of insights and did not really understand his message, and because of shallow sympathizers, and also because of his enemies, his vision went unfulfilled. (Ramakrishna, though he transcended all spheres, was better positioned to accept everything and to integrate wisdom, devotion and knowledge completely and harmoniously.) You were, basically, just an ardent devotee of Siva. Still, you were brave enough to subject your devotion to the full power of knowledge. A warrior general at work. You turned the very strategies of 'others' against themselves, and to that extent you enjoyed your triumphs. But if you and Vallalar had acted in concert, his efforts would not have gone in vain. Your efforts too would have been victorious; they would not have lost their lustre and stagnated, as they seem today. That's what we think these days, Father. There was nobody at that point in time but Vallalar who would have helped you achieve your objectives, if only you had approached him with the attitude of accepting his abilities while not losing any of your own. But you were incapable of doing that. The Rev. Father Peter Percival showed his love for you, and because of that, he was able to make use of you; it is sad that you could not show Ramalingasamy your love in the same way. Oh Father, do not think we are simply finding fault with you. We accept your goals as our goals; it's just that that's how it seems to us from today's perspective. That is to say, if those things were to happen today and we were around, we would not have let them happen. That's the sense in which I feel pushed to point out these things. Although there were many other reasons as well that you and Vallalar did not join together, your narrow perspective was in large measure responsible: that is the thought that rises up in us. But whatever we feel, you cannot refute the truth of what we see today. Today Vallalar's efforts have failed, and your early victories, too, have lost their lustre and gone stagnant. Even today we remain pathetically amusing, with issues like 'temple entry', 'satyagraha', 'lockouts' and 'police brutality'. Now, if we claim that these dreamers in their sheds and these sloganeers roaming the streets are the fruits of those reforms that you refused to undertake, that you blocked, or that your narrow perspective simply would not permit you to undertake, would there not be at least an element of truth in that? That's how it strikes us in our state of affairs, Father. Those noisy sloganeers are trying to correct your mistakes—and the dreamers in their sheds are trying to forget your mistakes. Because you tried to envision all of literature and the arts within the Saivite fold you were unable to give your full support to other arts and literatures, and you let them go, and when you did that through your ignorance, you forgot all about true art and literature, Father. You forgot them and you denounced them, Father. You constricted the boundaries of art, Father. And that is why now, in this land where you tried to nurture Tamil and Saivism, instead of the arts it is only dreams that flourish. That is precisely why we feel that we have to remind ourselves over and over again, as though we were newly attempting to be civilized: 'Having a home is not enough to emancipate us—our lives must become a stage for wondrous plays and songs.' Moreover, while you wrote your condemnations of people from other religions, Father, you forgot all about the social reforms and the service to literature that the other religions had managed to accomplish. Now, to eradicate that mistake, political shops have opened their doors, one for every person, one on every street corner, hard-selling items of foreign production. This shouting and sloganeering in all the streets is just a part of that same sales campaign. However they, too, are unable to plumb the depths of our society. But look at us! We are organizing a Commemoration for you. In this context, organizing an event could easily become farcical—particularly so if we did not include a new agenda. It is precisely to establish this agenda that we are laying all these things out, in your august presence.

Father, here is our first appeal: You must bless us to instil henceforth, into everything and everywhere, the love that you showered upon Tamil, upon Saivism, and upon Siva. Siva is indeed everywhere. That love which we give to Siva must also become a love for everything that Siva creates, and which he himself becomes. Love is not attachment. It is an ecstasy that breaks attachments. True love will be born only after all attachments have been transcended. It must even transcend the attachment inherent in thinking that love is the only goal. When we say love alone is what is needed, if that turns into an attachment, it will turn itself into an impediment for that very love. Attachments are simply impediments to a great, expansive love. Thus with no special attachment to anything—even without loving the perspective called love—an ecstatic love that upholds wisdom must become our weapon. Love that upholds the wisdom of destroying our very own selves! (The all-transcending Buddha remains the embodiment of total love!) Through such a love, unattached to anything and accepting and nurturing everything, the love that upholds wisdom must be what Siva means to us. You must grant us that; it is our first appeal.

We bring up our agenda in the very fundamentals of that appeal. This is what it is. In Jaffna where you nurtured Saivism and Tamil, the religion of humanity and equality also must henceforth thrive. All efforts must be made so that it will thrive. That is next on our agenda, which we lay out in your august presence. We will also set out action plans for this in your august presence, but now first, we are standing here as we ask for your blessing.

Now, I wonder what you think of all this. But you must understand that certainly, in one stroke, we have brought you together with Vallalar Ramalingasamy of Vadalur. Yes, as far as we are concerned, you were not two separate people. Just two sides of the same trajectory. You didn't realize it back then. Maybe it was the compulsions of your time, or rather your perspective on it, that made it impossible for you to see that. But now we understand, and we understand your failure to realize it. However, henceforth you should understand it yourself. That also is our request. Further, if today you were to wear the 'Navalar' costume that you wore from 1822 to 1879, that would in truth be the kind of blasphemy against Siva that you yourself condemned. We would like to tear up the various costumes that you have worn. It is your august presence beyond these costumes which we seek and touch through these appeals. Even if other people do not understand this, we are sure you will. Some might think that you did what you did as a simple, human individual, but did you think that? Did you not live your life in the belief that in your state of complete surrender it was god alone who worked through you, that it was all god's doing? If not, would you have determined to die if you lost your court case in Chidambaram? He is the one who did it all, and he will also be the one who saves us all. If not, you were prepared to make your death a sacrifice, to actually annihilate yourself, were you not? Isn't that so, Father? Just as that very god goaded you into a life of service, did he not also melt Ramalingasamy's heart and cause him to overflow with grace, and to sing? Had you turned the love you held for Siva and for Saivism to Ramalingasamy as well, might you not have seen god in him, too? That, Father, is what we want to do. That same love, that grand love, that upholds wisdom, that is what we are going to turn for everywhere; we will go everywhere in search of it. In twisting and searching for that great light we will see the omnipresent lord himself.

Jaffna henceforth should become the birthplace of the search for that great light. It should become the abode of that inner light, its wellspring. In the cast of that inner light not only Ramalingasamy but also everyone he tried to seek out and embrace, like Buddha, and Krishna, and so many other people, need to be praised and embraced. And not only they but Marx, Lenin and Mao Zedong also need to be realigned from this proper perspective. That is our request and our agenda: we submit these things in your august presence. But what we are looking for in your august presence is not just the usual holy-man 'Navalar' part that you play. We are going way beyond that costume, searching for the one who is always everywhere and in everything, the one who causes all things to act—he is the one we are searching for. In fact it is really him to whom we submit our petitions and our agenda, through you. To a son of the true tradition of Jaffna you are but a means to help in the search for that almighty one.

~

Father, there is this image that arises in my heart along with my thoughts about you, but is it true?

I really don't know. It is that picture of you that we see in all the books—wearing your dhoti, adorned with a shawl, with stripes of sacred ash all over your body, sitting with an open book in your hand—that's how I see you as well. That may well be the appearance you presented for Tamil and for Saivism. In preparing for the festival, I thought about displaying a picture of you; so I searched all over town—Jaffna town. 'If it were not for Navalar from Nallai town, where would Tamil be? Where would music be?'—in the Jaffna that praises you this way and is organizing a festival in your honour, I could not find a single picture of that Navalar from Nallai town. I went from shop to shop but I could not find you. True, you are not for sale. Still, it seemed a real shame that in shops where I could see pictures of the god you worshipped, your picture was not there. The anger that rose in that disappointed heart flowed out onto a different picture, one which was hanging everywhere: Sri Sathya Sai Baba!

Well, it's unfair to think you might know this character. He is my contemporary. Tight, billowing curls of hair that stand up like steel wool, a long, flowing, red silk shirt, a glistening gold neck chain that hangs down to his chest, and a little smile—and with all this his fair skin. Holy man Sri Sathya Sai Baba! He hangs there in shop after shop. I guess he is the avatar for this kali yuga. Om Sri Sri Sri Sathya Sai Baba! Om Sri Sri Sri Sathya Sai Baba! Om Sri Sri Sri Sathya Sai Baba! If you pray and write it down on postcards this way and mail it to twenty people, you will get everything you wish for. Om Sri Sri Sri Sathya Sai Baba!

But really, I did not write this to make you smile, or for your merriment. I just want to show you how things felt to me when I got mad and disappointed because I could not find your picture. Actually, I neither love nor loathe Sathya Sai Baba. I don't have the mindset that says religious devotion flourishes only if you make sacred ash and bananas materialize out of thin air. So I have listened to the stories that circulate about him, but I have kept my distance. Only time will tell whether or not he really is an avatar—or some other avatar could tell. So, up to that point I neither accepted him nor denounced him. But at that moment, when I could not find your picture, I did, in my heart, denounce him.

Lies, utter lies! Not just him, but those shops that sold his picture, and today's consumerist culture that fosters such shops, all felt like lies and fakes. Lies and fakes!

That's when it struck me. I felt that I saw right then the meaning of that little bud of a smile on that face with flowing hair.

'Lies and fakes—that's me, Sai Baba, too, right? Who dares to have the gold and silks that I do not have? Who encompasses the lies and tricks that god does not encompass? Lies and fakes—that's me, too.'

That was the answer that my heart handed me, given my reading and my experience up to that point. In that state of mind, I felt that I really understood Sai Baba. In the same way it felt like I really understood that in this day and time it is not enough to show off a body adorned with holy ash.

Father, a while ago I asked if you could accept and embrace those dream-lovers clowning around in their sheds and those faction-lovers shouting slogans as they roam the streets—do you remember? Maybe that is something you cannot do. But there has to be someone who can do it. For the compulsions of our times we need someone like that. I am not saying it is Sathya Sai Baba. But through him I have discerned the characteristics of the guru I seek. What we need these days is a saint who can instil wisdom not only in all departments of society, not only in all the labours of society, but even into deceit, theft, prostitution, and all the other illusions, someone who will accept everything, and reform it. Only that kind of an expansive spirituality will be of help in this age. The end of kali yuga must come about in this way.

Father, why has your face darkened? It seems like you have not even read the last bits that I wrote. An avatar of god! Are those words so terrifying?

Dear Father, if the roles you played, and your attitudes, were appropriate to the demands of your time, then they will be appropriate for all time, and they will determine whether your loving face should be forgotten or darkened. Okay, I am not trying to make you accept anything I insist on. We just wish to spread our principles out and dedicate them to your august presence, and we seek your blessings. Your unbounded love will not pass us by without illuminating us. We have faith in that. So now I want to say this as well: We totally believe that god (Siva) will be born as a human avatar. In this sense we are not only Vaishnavas, but Christians as well. You see, Dear Father, could that be the only thing that god cannot do? If we were to define him as incapable of that, would we not be trying to constrict him within our own boundaries?

Ramalingasamy asked, 'How would a name make a difference to madmen, anyway?' Didn't he? We would like to raise this question in a different form: 'For a mad man, what physical appearance would be impossible, or not to his liking?' Father, that is precisely why, as a thoroughgoing Saivite myself, I accept this madman and I worship him. At the same time, as a Buddhist I reject him. As a Muslim, I see him only as the one who is utterly beyond all this crazy costumery. As a Vedantin I call him an illusion, and I call him yet another form within that illusion. And he is universal, I say. And the universe is Brahma, I say. For such a great man, who puts on the appearance of a madman, what could ever be impossible, Father? At the same time, Father, would he not be capable of standing as everything? Have you read the Gita and appreciated it? I like it a lot. In the Gita, god says, 'I will appear to you in any way you wish to see me.' That is the first thing a person who believes in equality must understand. A man who understands that will accept everything, and he will move beyond everything as well. That is exactly what we wish for, Father.

Father, we would like to emphasize one thing here, now, at the end. Please do not jump to the conclusion that we are insulting the principles that you cultivated, or that we are simply laying out before your holy presence those vulgarities you condemned. It could well be that people might come to you and complain about me along exactly those lines. Father, I am just a child of that Tamil tradition that you fostered. It is simply with that understanding, and at the urging of that understanding, that we express all these things. But with the passage of time, our objectives have matured as well. We are trying to spread this tradition as one that belongs to all nations, yet without doing damage to the Saivism and the Tamil that you cultivated. It is not enough, Father, for our tradition to stop with Jaffna. Our problems today are of a different sort. We must be held accountable for every bomb that explodes far away, for every war that is waged, and for every event that occurs. And we must demonstrate how to bring all that to an end. If we do not, our silence will destroy us. It will aid in the destruction of the whole world. All of that has become our own lives' problems today. Given that situation, if we chatter on about praising your tradition, simply apply some holy ash to our bodies and go on with our lives, we will in fact, Father, be killing both you and your tradition. Turning ourselves into trained teachers or graduates, dreaming of going into medicine or engineering, calling ourselves scholars and pundits, thinking mostly about our survival, living for ourselves and our own troubles—that is what the highest token of your tradition has come to, Father. We can't even resolve neighbourhood temple disputes and caste conflicts. We are crippled. With this helplessness and selfishness of ours, your tradition also is dying a crippled death. In such a state, leaving aside international problems, when some among us really need to call upon distant gods like Marx and Mao Zedong to address the problems of our very own society, is it their fault? Don't we have to admit that they, at least, do not shut their eyes and forget their own dreams—that they continue in their search? In this state of affairs, Father, we are beginning to search for a way to revitalize your tradition and through it—through it!—to solve not only our own problems but also international ones. This is something you should not lose sight of. Today there are still some oldsters who preserve the past as it was done in the past. They make the claim that they are your direct descendants. Father, do not think that we are competing with them. If we were compared to them, in their eyes, we would be tiny wisps of straw. We admit that. But even a tiny stick of straw, if it receives grace and strength in the presence of a mighty person, can turn to steel, can it not, Father? All that those oldsters preserved could become a background from which to surge forward, could it not, Father? This we surrender in your presence, and ask for your grace. You must give us your grace and your blessing.

We will write more at another time.

With love,
Nachiketan

(Written by Thalaiyasingam under the pen name Nachiketan, just before his death in 1973, having come to know about plans to organize a centenary for Navalar.)

Translated by D. Senthil Babu

Thalaiyasingam, *'Sree La Sree Arumuga Naavalarku Ezhudhum Vinnappam'*, in Mu. Ponnampalam (ed.), *Thalayasinkam Padaippukal*, Kalachuvadu, Nagerkovil, 2006, pp. 771–783

Oh Driver

Neelavanan

oh . . . oh . . . driver
drive the cart drive

we're headed for a new town
before the sundown

oh . . . oh . . . driver . . .

in the flowers and gardens, all over the fields
a lovesoaked song
together until our journey is ended
we will keep walking along.

oh . . . oh . . . driver . . .
even before the path disappears
in the sorrowful teardrop sea of the fog
even before the moon's sickened shadow
behind us begins to follow along . . .

Oh . . . oh . . . driver . . .

Translated by Rebecca Whittington

Neelavanan, '*O . . . O . . . Vandikkara*' (1970s), in M.A. Nuhman and A. Jesurasa (eds.), *Patinoru Eelattu Kavingargal*, CreA, Chennai, 1984, p. 81

Walk

Mu. Ponnampalam

I'm walking with a friend
an evening of threadbare sun
in front of us the darkness breathing
scattered by the wind's sneeze
the feathers of darkness spread all over the sky
I'm walking with a friend.

the bamboo thatched forest road
nevertheless
human
mouths' lost speech sounds—
a little village, towering
mountains all around
tunnelling through them
feet go floating, by
way of that ever open forest road.

a roaring sound
a bridge, below it drawn
out of the forest the river's little wail
branching off—
the arm-wearying thought of love?
stroking the full-bodied tender shoots
the disembodied wind rolling along!

is the road still growing?
the road buries itself in darkness
yet—
the song of the diverging branches
can still be heard.

Translated by Rebecca Whittington

Mu. Ponnampalam, '*Natai*' (1970s), in Mu. Ponnampalam, *Kaalil Leelai*, Dhwani, Chennai, 1997, pp. 90–91

Yesterday Evening, This Morning

M.A. Nuhman

yesterday evening
we were here.

through the crowded streets of the city of Yaazh
through the traffic jam
we went pushing our bicycles.

we stood in front
of the Bhupala Singam bookstand.
we flipped through the magazines.

we were looking
at the crowd of people at the bus stop.
various faces
various colours
coming going
getting on and off
we saw them leaving.

we went walking up to the market
past the statue of Tiruvallavar
crossing the post-office junction
we took a breath of air in Pannaiveli.
at the kiosk
right by the 'Regal'
we drank tea and smoked cigarettes.

we watched
Jack London's
'Call of the Wild'.

in a wind that ruffled our hair
climbing onto our bicycles
we went back home.

so this morning dawned.
in the city streets we had been walking
rifles were roaming in khaki uniforms
bullets were raining down.
boring into bodies
they were drinking souls.

even the bus stop had died
the city lost the smell of humans.
the shops lay burning and smoking
like buildings felled by bullets
the old market lay in ruins
in every street
lay burnt, charred tires.
this is how
we lost
life today.
this evening
we lost.

Translated by Rebecca Whittington

M.A. Nuhman, *'Nerraiya Malaiyum Inraiya Kaalaiyum'* (1977), in *Alai* Journal, Jaffna, December 1977, pp. 239–240

Your Plight Also

A. Jesurasa

you may be returning from the beach
or you may be returning home
from the theatre

sudden sound of a gunshot
followed by the sound of hurrying boots.
you, having died,
will lie fallen in the street
a knife will sprout in your hand;
a gun will sprout too!
you will make your name
as a 'terrorist'
no one can question anything.

frozen silence;
but
in the hearts of the people
rage rises.

Translated by Rebecca Whittington

A. Jesurasa, *'Unnudaiyavum Kathi'* (1979), in M.A. Nuhman and A. Jesurasa (eds), *Patinoru Eelattu Kavingargal*, CreA, Chennai, 1984, p. 179

(The backdrop to this poem is the emergency that was declared in Jaffna, in the Northern Province, from July to December 1979.)

Journey

S. Sivasegaram

the weakness of daylight the strength of the darkness
the night triumphs once again.
flourishing trees, night drying out in the leaves
scorched, turned into charcoal.
swaying crown of a tall coconut
the ghosts stand shrunk with fear.
you can hear the little beetles crying out
the trembling of frogs' bodies.
the moon stumbles in the sky
falls into the pool of clouds and drowns.
darkness still surrounds.

a long journey lies ahead—
eyes turned blind
struggling feet search for a path
dawn may still break tomorrow
and the feet may move faster

if it's possible to go
just two steps beyond the darkness, I will.
will time stand still and wait for the dawn?

Translated by Rebecca Whittington

S. Sivasegaram, '*Payanam*', in M.A. Nuhman and A. Jesurasa (eds), *Patinoru Eelattu Kavingargal*, CreA, Chennai, 1984, p. 170

Hope

V.I.S. Jayapalan

like the sorrow
of a koel bereft of its lover
gently gently
the river seeps.
the *varaal* fishes jump
gasping for breath
among the reeds set dancing in the wind.
a summer evening.
next to me
on the warm white sand
I see
lying drying
rinds of banyan fruit
and five or six little seeds,
even though
somewhere far off in the distance
in a sweet voice
a Vanni boy
is singing of rain.

Translated by Rebecca Whittington

V.I.S. Jayapalan, '*Nambikkai*', in M.A. Nuhman and A. Jesurasa (eds), *Patinoru Eelattu Kavingargal*, CreA, Chennai, 1984, p. 186

Seashore

V.I.S. Jayapalan

the girl of time draws
with sand on the seashore
a poor girl.

before her the sea stretches out
behind the ancient sea
the sky continues
beyond the sky
she stands still to follow it with her eyes.

a fence of screw pine trees
in the distance a little hut;
inside the hut
a little child sleeping

in the rowboat dancing
in the deep sea
the surface wind comes carrying
the scent of screw pine flowers
winds, big winds
winds with pitch-darkness
the pitch-darkness trembling
many miles of sea swelling.

that night
of hands joined in prayer
at every little stone shrine
cannot be so quickly forgotten.

even after conquering the rolling seas
and bringing riches
this little hut,
two fistfuls of rice,
by the grace of the boatman
a twisted thought
a sigh.

the morning star only shines
in the sky
in life, it's just dark.

Translated by Rebecca Whittington

V.I.S. Jayapalan, '*Kadarpuram*', in M.A. Nuhman and A. Jesurasa (eds), *Patinoru Eelattu Kavingargal,* CreA, Chennai, 1984, p. 190

Unsung Songs

Shanmugam Sivalingam

the moment the flowers have budded
they wilt and fall.
the instant after conception
abortion.

even though young shoots
sometimes form stunted
all of a sudden
they are cast out
the stench of blood drifts in.
inside the egg a chick
dies with its just budding wings
but still
you tell me to sing.

in the street the corpses stink,
when the bullets broke the lock
the white doves fell head down
wings broken, and lie cruelly curled
the boys leave without telling us
they tell us to look for corpses on the shore
they tell us the corpses heaped on the shore
are the ones that were dumped in the sea
but still
you tell me to sing.

blood-curdling songs
songs of rotting corpses
songs of darkness
hanging overhead
like pitch-black smoke
without being aborted
without being stunted
without being cast out
a time will come
rending the heart
stumbling in the throat
exploding on the tongue

ask then—
not now.

Translated by Rebecca Whittington

Shanmugam Sivalingam, '*Paadatha Padalkal*' (1984), in Shanmugam Sivalingam, *Neer Valaiyangal*, Tamizhiyal, Chennai, 1988, pp. 112–113

Lankapuri Raja

Piramil

It was that unearthly hour after midnight, and Gopalakrishnan found himself awake—12:49 a.m.

The electronic wall clock, burning in the gleam of the night-light, announced the death of 1984 and the birth of 1985. The two dots between the 12 and the 49, like drops of blood one above the other, seemed to quiver on the point of disappearing.

Padmini and Abhiraman. The child Abhiraman had not even made it past the age of five when Padmini passed away from complications due to the miscarriage of her second pregnancy.

Thirteen years had already gone by, and like Padmini, Abhiraman had also vanished—but not into the realm of death. If that had been the nature of his disappearance, his memory, like Padmini's, would have merely brimmed up and subsided. By now Gopalakrishnan, a retired government surveyor, would have lost himself deep in his heaps of private land records.

Abhiraman was now barely seventeen. Once, while he was still a little child, Gopal and Padmini had been forewarned of this recent disappearance.

The incident took place in the town of Lankapuri in the Sinhala forest region—the memory hit Gopal with as much force as if it had happened yesterday. That day, while he was playing with the Sinhalese village children in the entrance to the survey tent, Abhi had dubbed himself Raja, King. According to the villagers' traditional belief, the Lankapuri Raja was an extraordinary elephant that reigned over this forest region. Elephants often came to the village attracted by the sugar cane fields, but none of them could withstand the villagers' intimidation tactics. The Lankapuri Raja was another matter altogether. He was never perturbed. Rising up on the horizon, he would stand towering above the sugar cane fields like an unshakeable mountain. Even so, he never ate more than a lorry-load of sugar cane, and he didn't often put in an appearance.

When the Raja did appear, either out of time-honoured custom or to test his authenticity, the villagers would set off firecrackers. At the sound of these firecrackers, any other tusker would turn tail and lumber off at top speed, but if it was the Raja himself, he would turn his magnificently curved, long tusks towards the noise and send an inquisitive look in the direction of the explosion. The villagers, taking notice, would crowd around to behold the king with fearful reverence. For all that, people took any smoky form far off in the distance to be the Raja. But for the Raja, the fireworks were a kind of ritual binding him and the village.

Padmini had shown the Raja three times to the child Abhi, and in certain peculiar mental states, Abhi had to be addressed as Raja, or else he would pick up and fling about anything and everything that came to hand. It was more or less this mental state that had seized Abhi on the day in question, and the incident that followed stirred up the whole village.

Abhi, who had been playing with the village children, strutted off in his shorts and vanished from Gopalakrishnan's sight. When Gopalakrishnan asked, 'Where's Abhi?' the children said, 'Raja has gone into the forest.'

Gopal was struck by the solemn tone in which the children said this. He came out of the tent, and his child was nowhere to be seen. Gopal crossed the road in the direction the other children were pointing and called out, 'Abhi! Abhi!' On the other side of the road, the densely thicketed forest began abruptly. The crowd of men and women that had gathered at the sound of Gopal's voice plunged into the thicket and spread out in all four directions in search of the child. Padmini stood terror-stricken in the road. The old Sinhala village headman Charles Udavatta admonished the crowd: 'Quiet down, don't make a racket.' Once he had imposed enough silence so that only his own voice could be heard, he called out in a mild voice, 'Raja!' At once, Abhi's shrill voice sounded out like an elephant's trumpet. Abhi was sitting beside the path that led to the sugar cane fields, endeavouring to extract, without tears, a thorn that had pierced the sole of his foot.

Now, twelve years after this event, Abhi had disappeared again. He had not bothered to get in touch with either his high school or his friends to find out if he had been promoted to the next grade.

The Sri Lankan political problem, which had reared its head many a time between father and son, seemed to be a clue to Abhi's disappearance. Abhi's view that the Sri Lankan Tamils could attain liberation from Sinhala military atrocities only through armed violence seemed to Gopalakrishnan just that of an unruly child. Abhi seemed to forget all about Lankapuri, the Sinhala forest village where he had grown up. After his mother's death in Colombo and his father's transfer to his hometown Triconamalai, the Lankapuri Raja that had once loomed so large in his thought was no longer part of Abhi's consciousness.

The childhood memory of the extraordinary experience of beholding the Raja had remained imprinted in Abhi's heart until the age of thirteen. Then one day Abhi asked his father how his mother had died. He didn't believe the story of the miscarriage; he declared: 'Amma was killed in Lankapuri village.' Gopal, disconcerted by this statement of Abhi's, pulled out the pile of papers containing Padmini's death certificate and slapped it down in front of his son, shouting, 'Look here, see for yourself.' But how many mothers, how many women had been disgraced and killed—when Abhi launched this next weapon against him, Gopal had nothing to say in return. This tender thirteen-year-old heart had seized up and turned to stone before it even ripened.

Gopal looked up at his son. Even at thirteen, Abhiraman, on his way to becoming the star soccer player in the eastern province school system, sported the build of a seventeen-year-old. His brows often furrowed in a secret sorrow that lent maturity to his childish eyes . . . A very close friend of Abhi's, Chandirasekaran, was a member of a Tamil family in Rattinapuri ravaged by Sinhala fanatics . . . His was one such tender heart that hardened into stone before it ripened on seeing his mother torn apart before his very eyes. This stony quality must have spread from Chandirasekaran's heart to Abhi's.

Gopal began to sense that, even at the age of thirteen, Abhi must be working out in some secret physical exercise programme. He witnessed in anguish a distant gaze brewing in Abhi's eyes by the age of sixteen. The child Abhi had at some point abruptly become a young man, and still Gopal could not see through to the bottom of this distant gaze. Shooting up unusually fast, as if goaded by his physical traits, Abhi had already reached his full adult height at sixteen. Then one day he took off on his bicycle, saying he would only go as far as the stadium and back. He never came back.

Even police Inspector Jayatilake said to Gopal as he searched Abhi's belongings for evidence, 'Don't get angry, Surveyor—if your child just had an accident somewhere, we'll be glad to let you know.' With that, though, he pulled out a number of books from inside Abhi's pillow, and placed them in front of Gopal. Amilcar Cabral, Frantz Fanon, Nelson Mandela—who were these writers?

'I'm no bookworm,' said the inspector. 'But I do have information about certain matters. These people are not writers. They're armed revolutionaries. According to our information, terrorists. All three of them Africans.'

Gopal did not rise up, but his eyes flared. His teardrops fell onto Cabral's bright smile, dampening the cover of the book.

At this point, Inspector Jayatilake, who had come across so amicably at first, began to lose patience and revealed his true colours. This policeman, who was supposedly trying to help Gopal find his son, now seemed to be asking, indirectly, 'Where is your son hiding?'

During that evil hour, Jayatilake appeared twice in uniform, his revolver drawn, with a jeepful of armed police behind him.

'As far as we are concerned, Abhiraman is not a child, Surveyor. He's a terrorist of the first order who trains directly with a character named Charles Anthony, here in Triconamalai. He would only come to you if he were mortally wounded. Recently there was a gunfight between the police and a gang of terrorists, so we came to find out what's going on.'

During this speech, Gopal stood aloof. After the policeman left, it took him two days to put the house back in order.

Now, there came a knock on the door at this unearthly hour of the morning, and he was reminded of the inspector's visit. But this was a different knock, a stealthy sort of knock. At first, Gopal heard the knock in his sleep and it woke him up, but once awake, he forgot why he had woken up. When the knock came again, he understood that this was what was waking him up. 12:49 a.m.

It couldn't be Abhi, or it must be Abhi. He would come home only if he is mortally wounded. Gopal, his body and mind trembling, got up and opened the front door without putting on the light. The realization that it was not Abhi produced at the same time a deep pain and a deep relief. Who was it?

In the darkness, all Gopal could see were the sharp eyes of a shortish figure.

'Who is it? What do you want?' Gopal asked in Tamil. The figure laughed strangely.

'Same old Gopal Mahatmiya, same old voice. I wish you a happy new year.'

Gopal put on the light. There stood, bag in hand, the old Sinhalese village headman of Lankapuri, Charles Udavatta. For the first time in twelve or thirteen years, Gopal encountered a drop of Lankapuri. He said, 'Come inside.'

Udavatta looked Gopal up and down, and said, 'Where's Abhirama Raja?'

Gopal said, 'First sit and rest a little. What are you doing here? On your way to Ceruvavilai?'

'That too, but I don't have much faith in that place. All that is a Sinhala trick to take the Tamilians' land. I've been to Bodh Gaya,' said Udavatta, mixing Sinhala and Tamil. Then he said in Tamil, 'I came mostly to see you and Abhi. Where is he?'

Gopal, hospitably sitting his guest down, and steadying himself at the same time, said, 'I've sent Abhi to study in Madras.'

'You did well. This Sri Lanka of ours is disintegrating. In fact, you could have gone with him. I knew all along that all this would happen.' With that, he looked at Gopal significantly. 'You know about the Lankapuri Raja, don't you? All the signs were there.'

'I don't understand,' said Gopal. 'This New Year, and the one before that too, there's been a curfew. Did you get off the bus and come straight here? How did you get my address?'

'That boy Piyadas who used to work for you, he's my son-in-law now. He fell in love with Nalani and married her, and they have a seven-year-old daughter. Nalani named the girl Padmini. And you ask how I got your address!' Charles Udavatta bit into the biscuit Gopal had served him. 'The world can go to rot, but you and I have stood shoulder to shoulder before the Lankapuri Raja. Don't you know that the Raja has reached the great nirvana?'

In plain speech, this meant that the elephant called Lankapuri

Raja had died. But, for the Lord Buddha and for all those who attain the status of *arhat*, death means reaching the great nirvana.

Gopal set the drink in his hand down on the table. 'Was the Raja that old?'

'Old? That elephant could have lived another five hundred years, such an awesome strength he had! He uprooted and hurled down a couple of hundred trees, a whole jungle in fact, in the course of a few sleepless days, before he disappeared!'

'Why? Had he gone mad or something?'

Charles Udavatta glared angrily at Gopal for a moment; the next moment, he burst out laughing. 'Mahatmiya, I told you, this was no elephant. He was more of a man than any man. How could he go mad? Let me tell you what happened—then you will understand why Sri Lanka is falling apart like this today.'

After a pause, Charles Udavatta began: 'You know Lalit Adulat Mudali, who's unleashing the Sinhalese army on the Tamils nowadays? He has an older cousin-brother, Cyril Tissanayakka. This Cyril took out a government contract to catch elephants, so he came to Lankapuri and set up a tent. None of this came out in the news.

'We villagers tried so many times to tell Cyril—don't go trying to catch elephants here. We said everything we could think of to make him understand that the Raja wouldn't allow it. Half the people in the village started to leave.

'But Cyril Tissanayakka didn't budge. One time he took a big rifle from under the table, aimed it at me, and shouted rudely, "Clean this out, old man." "*Chi*, what kind of a man are you?" I shouted back at him. I went straight to Nalani and Piyadas and arranged to send them to Colombo, but I didn't go myself—a few of us stayed put in Lankapuri.

'In the meantime, the elephant catchers spent thousands of rupees chopping down gigantic trees and planting them in curved rows in the forest, so that if the elephants went inside, they wouldn't be able to get out. What could we do? The elephant catchers crushed all opposition from us Lankapuri folks. When we told them about the Raja, they said, "He's just a beast like any other that stands there in the fields and eats the sugar cane, isn't he? We'll catch him too, and then you can grow your sugar cane in peace." They told us all kinds of barefaced lies about Cyril's rifle.

'Within a month, the drums began to sound. Catching the scent of the elephant herd, the catchers stationed kettledrum players here and there to beat their drums, and the rest of them stood in rows in the bushes and made a racket to drive the elephants out. Sure enough, according to Cyril's plan, the elephants went running into the cage and stood there trapped by the huge arches of that cage. The elephant catchers explained their method: they would trap the elephants, leave them there to starve for a while, and then tame them with food. But the Lankapuri Raja was not among the herd—only the villagers knew that.

'That night, the elephants started trumpeting. After half an hour or so, a sudden silence fell. The elephant catchers were stumped by this silence—according to their calculations, the elephants should have kept trumpeting for days on end until they wore themselves out. In the middle of the night, the men who were guarding the elephant cage started shouting and came running back to town like wounded dogs. We managed to make out from their babbling that a gigantic elephant, an elephant as tall as two elephants, was standing outside the cage, uprooting the tree-arches and hurling them away.

'Far off on the edge of the forest, you could hear the sound of a mountainous form angrily gnashing its teeth—the sound of trees snapping. Some of us who knew our way around the forest took an alternative path to see what was going on.

'Dark in the darkness, the Raja was breaking down the elephant cage. He had to reach the central part of the cage and break four or so of the arches, each of them a giant tree that had been felled and shifted by means of gigantic machines. When we came to look, the first arch had already been broken down to the breadth of two elephants. It was three o'clock in the morning and the Raja's anger was storming in the wind. We got scared and ran back home to the village.

'At first, Cyril Tissanayakka didn't bother his head about this. He figured that even if the elephant broke one of the arches and went inside, it would get trapped in the arches of the tree-fence that had been driven in on both sides and be forced into the centre of the trap. That was what his experience told him.

'A couple of days went by. The sound of snapping trees stopped short. Nobody dared to go into the forest to scout out what had happened. Now the elephants started trumpeting again. Cyril, assuming that the giant elephant must have gotten trapped, started up the machines again to rebuild the broken fence. It was time for one of the machines to start picking up the huge whole trees that had been flung haphazardly here and there. Eleven o'clock. Suddenly, a trumpet very close by. Cyril Tissanayakka got out of his jeep and stood there, watching. The Raja burst out from some hiding place in the thick of the trees and came running towards the machine. Cyril ran and climbed into his jeep. The Raja came charging with lowered head and thrust his tusks right into the track wheels of a German machine built like a battle tank and as big as a house. The Raja lifted it up and tossed it on its side with one kick. With a meaningless roar, the machine grotesquely toppled over onto its back. Then the Raja turned and headed straight for Cyril Tissanayakka. Cyril couldn't get the jeep to start, so he grabbed the rifle beside him, jumped out of the jeep, and took off running. At that moment, we understood why the Raja had stopped halfway in breaking down the trap: his real aim was to destroy those who had caused it.

'Cyril saw the Raja heading straight for him. Planting a knee on the ground like a soldier, crouching and aiming the rifle at the centre of the Raja's forehead, he pulled the trigger twice. The rifle sound burst out with a crack like stone splitting. Instantly, two red spots appeared on the Raja's forehead. Cyril straightened his rifle and stood up. Like the machines, his rifle had been specially ordered from Germany; its bullets could hit a target a quarter of a mile away, and it was fitted with a telescope—so Cyril Tissanayakka stood up, sure that the bullets had pierced into the elephant's brain. At this point the elephant should have folded his knees, slumped down, and fallen to the ground. But that idiot Cyril didn't have the sense to realize that this was no elephant. The bullets that had entered the Raja's brain didn't slow him down in the least; in two steps he reached Cyril's side. Cyril's arms and legs grew numb; only his mouth screamed out in fear. The next moment, destruction. A week later, Cyril Tissanayakka's relatives gathered him up in two plastic buckets and took him away.

'Once he had Cyril destroyed, the Raja never broke his stride, but headed straight for the trap. Our hair stood on end as we watched from our hiding place. The Raja began to break down the trap again, tree by tree, and hurl the trees aside. Each tree collapsed under the Raja's assault in the space of two or three minutes. Streaming blood from the spots in the middle of his forehead, the Raja continued his battle. We watched for a long time, and we began to get hungry and thirsty. The elephant catchers had long since taken to their heels, and only we Lankapuri folks were left. We turned back to the village as the evening darkened. The cruel sound of trees snapping could be heard all night long. In the morning, we got up and quickly gulped down some bread and bananas, and then went out again to watch the Raja's tireless struggle. By now, his entire forehead was one cloud of blood. The point of one tusk had cracked off. At the place where the tusks entered the mouth, the blood had blackened. I broke down in tears.

'That day I stuck it out there until evening without even drinking a drop of water—but I didn't even feel the time pass. Once the Raja had gone straight to the centre of the cage, where we could no longer see him, we went back to the village.

'That night I woke up to the sound of the Raja's trumpeting. A terrible pain like two tusks seemed to shatter my head from inside my skull. I thought the trumpeting was some sort of hallucination, so I put a wet cloth on my forehead and tried to go back to sleep. My body was fiery hot, and began to tremble. Fever. I didn't even have Nalani nearby—somehow or the other I got back up and made myself an herbal decoction, then lay down again. That day the year 1982 ended and the year 1983 began. I know for certain that at the time I heard the trumpet, it was exactly twelve o'clock. My wall clock was striking twelve at that very moment. It was the timeless interval dividing two days, two years, two epochs. The Raja's trumpet rang out and disappeared into that empty space.

'The next day I stumbled over to look at the elephant cage. The tuskers and the female elephants and the baby elephants were all standing scattered outside the cage. I wandered into the midst of the trees and stood at the entrance to the broken cage. All four fences were broken down in one uniform line. The herd of elephants trapped inside had come out and was standing in the open, but the Raja's body was sitting there in the shade of the fence with its tusks pointing up toward the sky, like a statue of an excellent god. His right tusk was shattered, and his tusks and his whole head were one cloud of blood. My own body too lost its strength all of a sudden and I collapsed. If the village boys had not carried away my unconscious body, I would have died peacefully then and there. After that, a new and terrible epoch began. July 1983. I was witness to the rowdy armies of both Cyril Mathew and Gemini Tissanayakka tearing the Colombo Tamils into tiny shreds. It was my fate to be in Colombo then, to see those demons face-to-face. With the same eyes I took to Bodh Gaya for *darshan*, I was forced to see the full form of human cruelty. That's divine logic.'

Though Udavatta's voice had not once broken, from time to time his face crumpled. Tears went streaming from his eyes, ascending and descending the creases in the flesh of his face like the irregular surface of a craggy landscape. Gopal, too, however much he tried to contain his tears by straining his forehead, he could not. Looking reverently at the shattered face in front of him, he started to say, 'I didn't send Abhirama Raja to Madras. In reality he . . .'

Udavatta interrupted, 'I knew that even before I knocked on your front door.' He rubbed his face with his hands. 'I'm not crying only for the Lankapuri Raja. When I got off the bus, the police were stopping everyone and interrogating them before sending them on their way. As soon as I said your address, I alone got the royal treatment. They took me straight to the police station in a jeep and took down everything I said. One inspector told me about Abhirama Raja in a roundabout way. He asked me to spy on you and find out about him, and they brought me here in a jeep. This is why we call these Sinhalese morons. They've sent me to spy on you. I have only one thing to say to you: I've been on a pilgrim's journey to seek out everyone I know, pin them down, and tell them in person the story of the Lankapuri Raja.

'Abhiraman was born in Lankapuri, and his own journey is not at all far from the Raja's dharma.'

Translated by Rebecca Whittington

Piramil, '*Lankapuri Raja*' (23 June 1985), *Tinamani Katir*, Chennai; in K. Subramaniam (ed.), *Piramil Pataippukal*, Adaiyalam, Puthanatham, 2003, pp. 101–111

In the Evenings

Sivaramani

in the evenings
all burdens grow heavier.
when light and heat
inescapably chafing
against each other
on the dead daytimes
disappear
like words scrawled on a slate
and wiped away without a trace
I count my breaths
as I let them out—
not only to pass the time.

beside the light
the winged mites were falling down dead, one by one.
what should I count—
the winged mites?
or the stars that give out
unelucidated meanings
like the eyes
of the fallen?

I don't know the truths;
to spot the lies
in this darkness is not an easy task—
but

I can't ask my younger sister
who is studying for a test:
look for meanings in the things you do—

on the whole
everyone is in some sort of hurry.
for me
only memories remain.
outside,
the shadows of trees
that stand in tensionless silence
are torn down.

when dogs bark
suffering and tense
in the street
at the time when everyone goes to sleep
after checking the locked doors
one more time
I
cannot think
about the sun that will appear tomorrow.
to me this night is significant.
this darkness
where yet another friend
might be lost
like yesterday
is worth much to me.

Translated by Rebecca Whittington

Sivaramani, '*Maalai Nerangalil*' (1989), in *Sivaramani Kavithaigal*,
Women's Study Circle, Batticaloa, 1993, pp. 39–41

I Don't Have the Words

Sivaramani

I
don't have the words
to voice beliefs and solutions
like a pamphlet.

night;
day commanded by the night;
to me who doubts even
that tomorrow morning
the sun will rise
dreams
have lost their meaning.

when guns are thrust
at society's birth cord
the dream of a butterfly
that might sit
on the soft edge of a flower
is nothing to me
but an irrelevant occurrence.

in my efforts to live as a human being
I would like to leave the flowers on the trees.
to me
the beautiful night given form by day
is a dream.

Translated by Rebecca Whittington

Sivaramani, '*Ennidam*' (1989), in *Sivaramani Kavithaigal*, Women's Study Circle, Batticaloa, 1993, p. 38

My Lineage and I

Sivaramani

in this darkness
that is searching for everything
it is now certain there is absolutely nothing.

in the space crossed
by all the lines of descent
behind me
even I am left behind.

in the expanse
where heaven and hell
have been effaced
my feet have sunk
in unfathomable mud.

everybody
bears their own coffin
but eats their meals too
every mealtime.

even the space, the time, and the teachings
of the gods' messenger, the preacher
and the prophet
have been effaced.

no one has
anything like the joy
that might uplift
our stooping
times.
in an extraordinary effort
to bring everything
back to normal
among the sleeping and the dying

with my beliefs
I
am failing.

Translated by Rebecca Whittington

Sivaramani, '*Enathu Paramparaiyum Naanum*' (1989), in *Sivaramani Kavithaigal*, Women's Study Circle, Batticaloa, 1993, p. 42–43

Place: Jaffna University Canteen
Time: 4.30 p.m.

Sivaramani

like a lonely
little railway station
ignored and without passengers,
in the midst of everyone
between the compound walls
that rise along with laughter

one evening . . .

I was talking
with my friends.
the times
we like to be happy
in the middle of many wounds
not worthy of mention
without words to speak with

tapping out a forgotten song,
a friend and his fingers,
drops of tea
scattered on the long table . . .
the flies get caught
in cobwebs up there . . .

shrugging her shoulders my friend
laughed inside herself
who cracked the joke?
I don't know

the clouds moving slowly
over the glass roof-tiles
along with them the hour and minute,
the table and chairs
left standing without a trace of scent—
leaving the empty cups . . .
coming in through the door
the rays of the western sun
were chasing us
we got up—

not to change the world,
just heading for another night.

Translated by Rebecca Whittington

Sivaramani, *'Thanithu'* (1989), in *Sivaramani Kavithaigal*, Women's Study Circle, Batticaloa, 1993, p. 46–47

Summer Scorches Day after Day . . .

Su. Vilvarathinam

summer scorches day after day
even the water in the deep well has dried up
the bucket goes in, comes up empty
summer scorches day after day

not a spot of cloud in the sky
the bald trees suffer, extending their fingers into arid space
like men of withered dreams
summer scorches day after day

look at men wandering
shadeless shadowless
their footprints lost
crossing the path of my eyelids
in all directions the eye throws out
there are only hands stretched out to offer mirages
not one hand bears them
water, life
summer scorches day after day

fires burn all around
self-immolations
raw flesh
raw feelings
dreams of rawness
burn; charred

the very earth burns to a corpse
in the mirage
the shadow of fire falls
on the future—
glimmering like a shed snakeskin . . .
summer scorches day after day

in the scorching summer sun
even birds' shadows suffer
beneath bald trees
humanity is hunched, crouched
in the monstrously extended desert
its life parched
by the long-unbreathing wave of wind

is there anyone
waiting
though the heart be wrung out
for a drop of life-water
though the back be broken
for vertebrae to be handed out as crutches
on this long-drawn-out desert road
is anyone there
anyone at all . . .

Translated by Rebecca Whittington

Su. Vilvarathinam, '*Oru Paalaiyin Kural*' (1989), in *Uyirtthezhum Kaalathirkaga*, Vitiyal, Coimbatore, 2001, pp. 157–158

Time Will Write a Song for You

S. Ranjakumar

Today, the first bath in many days. Today's sun rose with a new look. Strange, without a hint of the overly warm dawns you expect in the month of Cittirai, but rather as if giving off just a touch of coolness. A coolness that creeps in, among the roots of our hairs, tingling.

In the early sunlight, unfurling their long, dew-strewn leaves, the tobacco plants emerged into view. Water pumps were spitting out a rapid, heavy flow of water. The sweet, heady pungency of tobacco mingled with the smoke of burning kerosene; they blended into a single fragrance.

The idea came to Arul first. He got up suddenly and went over and squatted down, without even taking off his shirt, and let the water pour over his head. Everyone turned and looked questioningly at Konamalai. Why were Konamalai's eyes so red all the time? Anger and pride always seemed to be gleaming between his tightly sealed, thin lips. His face had a strange, hard sheen, like black granite.

This morning Konamalai laughed with those red eyes of his. With fatherly tenderness, he watched Arul sticking his head into the cascading stream of water like a little kid.

'One gets to bathe, at last.'

Appa! What voice is that? Coming from someone who hardly spoke, there was great emphasis in every syllable.

Michael sat down.

Konamalai, Kedari, Periyannan, Perumal, Yosef, Anbarasan, then him . . . they all headed for the roaring water pumps.

Michael just sat there, waiting to collect the tactical information.

People looked at them once. Then, shaking their heads, they continued on their way. A little boy, around ten or eleven, came running towards them, shaking a soap box. He stood there with his hand stretched out. They kept washing themselves without paying him any heed.

Konamalai looked up. The boy's eyes were pleading, 'Take it . . . Take it . . .'

'Arul, get the soap.'

Arul began to grin through the soap suds foaming all over his head, navel, thighs, the soles of his feet. Arul was something of a joker. He told him all his secrets. One time he and Arul doubled up on a bicycle to go somewhere on an urgent errand. As they rode past a house rising sombrely behind a stretch of high land bordered by balsam trees in bloom, Arul gave him a thump in the ribs.

'That's my girl's house!' he whispered into his ear.

'. . .'

'What's it like . . . ?'

'A house . . . It's not bad at all . . .'

'You haven't seen her . . . if you'd seen her you'd know . . .'

'. . .'

'Hm . . . If everything ends well . . . If I'm even alive . . .'

'If . . . ?'

'Hm.'

He turned and looked up at Arul's face. For a second he saw all the splendours of the world flowering in Arul's tense face. He let out a sigh for Arul.

Only a moment!

Then Arul changed. The old tension in his eyes came back. He started pedalling the bicycle at high speed. A real hard worker!

A long time later. Today, a rare feast. From what a gifted

woman's hands! Fragrant cooking. Scooping and slurping up the food, Arul looked at him with a wink and a grin.

Every woman's cooking has its own taste. Even so, no one can match the taste of a mother's simple cooking. If Amma gives you plain hot water, it has a special taste. When the gentle darkness gathered, Amma would come home by way of the temple. It was all those gods she worshipped who forced her into her white widow's sari; then they watched her in spiteful silence. Every evening, with the back of her white sari wet with the water dripping from her hair after she doused her head and pulled up her damp hair, Amma would set out looking for Amman temples. When she came home, a whiff of camphor would come from Amma's body. As if Amman had come to infuse herself in Amma's persona, terrible and beautiful to see.

Amma didn't eat any meat or fish. After dark, she lit a stove of baked brick and cooked her food separately. How is it possible for Amma, who ate very little, and only once a day, to bustle about attending to so many tasks! Overcooked, starchy rice gruel and a thin curry with some lightly fried vegetables. Without fail, a crunchy *appalam*.

Amma could cook a meal in a second. He would wait with his mouth watering. Amma was about as tall as his shoulder. She had the colour and the coolness of a sliced cucumber. She must have been a great beauty back then. Is that why she had so many children? Even at this age, with her skin dry and her pace slackened, Mother's eyes give out a bright light.

He would get up and stand proudly, looking at his mother with a tender smile. Mother would throw back her head and daub sacred ash on his forehead.

'*Ammale*! . . .' Whenever he heard his mother's intimate, entreating voice, he would simply melt. And the lingering scent of burning camphor too, warm and moist—when mother touched his forehead, he would thrill at the scent that filled his nose. Mother's breath would touch his chest for a moment and move away. He would immediately be seized with hunger!

Sulochana Akka cooked in a hurry. She was in a hurry with everything. Whatever did she see in her dear husband? She would swoon like a snake at the sound of a snake-charmer's flute. Akka turned out so many dishes like so many children. If she put too much salt in one, another would have no salt at all. Only fish curry did she make properly—everything mixed together to give birth to a truly unprecedented taste.

He couldn't even remember the last time he went to Sulo Akka's house. Her husband, muttering to himself, would suddenly turn his face away and leave. He was a proper water buffalo. When he wasn't playing cards or slogging away at work, what did he do with his time except drink? He was good at making a mother out of Sulo Akka, though, every year, without fail. Sulo Akka had become like an eggplant, her eyelids cracked and her chest shrunk. Her husband was mumbling something or the other. Let him go! He only came to see her, anyway.

'Unnecessary problems for us . . .'

On his way out, her husband started to cackle. Akka bit her tongue and dragged him into the kitchen. She would not let go of his hands; she kept gripping them tight.

'Did you eat yet . . .' she asked, eager to nourish him. Not finding the strength to look up, he sat down silently. Akka briskly set out the food. She started to put morsels of food into his hands.

He could hear Akka sniffling.

'Amma quit going to the temple . . .'

'. . .'

'Amma has even given up going to the temple . . .' In the strength of her emotion, his sister's voice broke and started to squeak.

He shook off her hand and abruptly turned to leave.

'Wash your hands before you go . . .' Akka called out in a tearful voice. Unwilling to turn and look back, clenching his fists tightly over his palms, he went out as if he were ready to punch the wind.

He could hear the sound of Akka coming up behind him, calling out in a surge of emotion. He felt like plugging up his ears.

'From this moment on I won't go into any house,' he swore to the wind.

One time they broke down the big bridges on all four main roads.

Konamalai separated the men into groups. He got the north road. In a panic, people rushed to fill in the pits, using tractors to bring in dirt and gravel.

His watch! He stood there ready, looking all around him, an agile man with a big responsibility. The vans and buses reduced their loads and descended slowly into the pit.

Somebody gently took hold of his elbow.

He turned to look.

Sundari Akka!

Limping Sundari Akka! Sundari Akka, who caught the bus at sunrise to go to work. Would Amma be standing there still, staring anxiously at the doorway? If it weren't for this lame leg, wouldn't Indiran, Chandiran and all the other boys be waiting in line behind Sundari Akka? She had a set routine: she caught the bus at sunrise, went to work, and got home after dark.

Sundari Akka, standing there staring at him . . . He pretended to be distracted and looked off somewhere else. The bus was slowly making its way down into the lowland. Sundari Akka came and stood even closer to him. Opening her handbag, she took out a few notes and stuffed them into his pocket. He stuffed them back into her hands. She looked at him helplessly.

'Keep it, man . . .'

'I don't need it . . . I don't need anything . . .'

Sundari Akka looked him up and down. From his matted hair to his feet that had wandered in the sun and the rain, he was covered in red dust. He had tied his lungi so high his thighs were showing. The shoulder seam of his shirt had come apart.

'Couldn't you at least buy a shirt . . .'

'. . .'

'Keep it, man . . .'

'There . . . Look . . . The bus is leaving . . .'

She had big eyes, Sundari Akka. She looked at him intently. She looked at him, wishing she could take him captive in her eyes. Two diamond drops slid down, dampening her cheeks.

Turning back time and again to look at him, Sundari Akka left. Limping, the last person to board, she got on the bus. She stood looking at him through the back window. He looked that way as if by chance.

He saw Sundari Akka's big eyes filling the entire back window. He suddenly turned the other way.

'I won't give my feelings any room,' he swore to the wind.

Today, extraordinarily, everything looked new. The cool wind embraced his freshly bathed body. He looked up at the sky. The brilliant blue sky of the month of Cittirai, with bales of cotton floating in it, was not to be seen today. Rain was in the air and the wind felt dense. Dark clouds were spreading slowly from the east.

Michael gave out the information.

'They said the stuff is coming by the south road . . . We are to go and take it over midway . . .'

Konamalai got up abruptly. Excited, he gave several orders in succession.

'Right, the south road!. Don't worry . . . We don't need heavy arms . . . One per person is enough . . .'

'Perumal, take the van . . . It looks like it's going to rain . . . We have to transfer the stuff without letting it get wet . . .'

'Yosef, you stay here . . .'

Perumal was a good driver; he'd studied every inch of the roads. Perumal could fly along roads with mines and potholes, turning sharply, without shifting gears.

Konamalai jumped up next to Perumal; next to him, Periyannan.

Him . . . Kedari . . . Arul . . . Anbarasan . . . Michael . . . they crowded into the back. He sat next to the door. Except for Perumal, everyone had 'the thing' clenched in their palms. They were ready.

Stirring up red dust, Perumal took off. The sky let out a roar.

A little ways ahead, they could drive up onto the main road. They had to make a sudden right-angle turn. Perumal got ready to shift gears. At the crossroads, a crowd of people were standing in the shadow of an old banyan tree. Perumal slowed down.

Their eyes were dazzled by a flood of light. A bolt of lightning came blazing down across the sky like a creeper. The sky roared again with a vengeance. Perumal hesitated. He stopped.

There was a crackling sound of something snapping and falling. People moved away, dispersed. One of the big branches of the banyan tree cried out 'Oh' and hit the ground.

Confusion spread over people's faces. Konamalai said, 'Go ahead.' Perumal planted his foot on the clutch.

A shrivelled old man, with his mouth dripping saliva, came in front of them, waving his hands.

'Sons . . .'

Konamalai looked at him as if to say, 'What?'

'Banyan trees aren't supposed to break and fall like that, sons . . . It's dangerous to travel now, sons . . .'

Arul let out a mocking laugh.

'We're in danger every second, Thatha!'

The old man looked at them with pity and regret.

Perumal easily made the turn up onto the main road. Once again lightning came crashing down on the horizon. The wind turned heavier. What is this? Today, everything was turning strange. From the south-east corner, forgetting that this was the month of Cittirai, the cold wind kept blowing, hard.

'Heavy rain's coming this way, Perumal . . . Quick . . .' Perumal pressed his foot down harder.

People were scurrying into their houses. An expression of welcome, eager and astonished, to the rain falling out of season showed on their faces. Standing in their entryways, they watched intently as their van went roaring off.

The rain began to fall in big, heavy drops. The windshield began to fog up. Like apparitions in a dream, the road and the trees took on a strange appearance. Perumal switched on the windshield wipers. They didn't work . . .!

Perumal wasn't one to give up easily. They were used to seeing through pitch-darkness like cats. He went on, looking sharply ahead.

What rain! A rain such as he had never seen in his life. The scent of settling dust grew stronger. He took in that scent joyfully. He put his feet up comfortably on the front seat.

Suddenly the road seemed desolate. Why? There was nobody around. Because of the rain, or what? Not one other vehicle came from the other direction. Except for an old bullock getting tirelessly drenched in the pouring rain. A desolate road.

Now the rain was like fierce, frenzied arrows inundating the earth. The sky gave frequent warnings with loud claps of thunder. Then lightning would strike, splitting the sky from top to bottom like a sharp sword.

For some reason their hair began to stand on end. They were used to withstanding more blood-freezing cold than this. But what's happened today? A cold that pierced through their bones to the marrow.

Arul rubbed his hands to warm them up. He folded his hands close up against his chest. Looking at him, he laughed with his natural friendliness. Today, for some reason, Arul was laughing more than normal. A strange light had come over Arul's face.

Suddenly, for some reason, the thought of Amma, Sulo Akka, Sundari Akka, all of them, rose in his mind.

Along with the rain, the camphor fragrance of Amma's body blew in. Who mixed camphor into the rain?

Sundari Akka's big eyes appeared before him, with two diamond drops of tears. It was as if she were touching his hands gently. Sundari Akka probably went to work even in this rain.

Sulo Akka's squeaking voice came too, mingled with the ghostly wind. Sulo Akka seemed to be calling him in unbearable frustration and overflowing love.

This One closed his eyes for a moment. He let out a long sigh, as if a cobra had taken shape in his heart and burst out, splitting his throat.

He opened his eyes. Perumal was comfortably making a turn without changing his speed. An expert, all right! With the heavy rain coming down in sheets, making it impossible to see for even a hundred yards, and the windshield wipers not working, he was driving the van along at high speed! Who else could do that? A genuine expert!

The road stretched ahead in a straight line. Perumal kept tearing along.

Why . . .? Why . . .? What . . .?

Perumal slammed on the brake. Everyone began to sense some demonic thing coming straight towards them.

Perumal turned and looked at Konamalai. Konamalai, his face tense, shook his head as if to say, 'Go on ahead.' Everyone felt they had to breathe fast. Everyone closed their fingers tightly over the palms of their hands.

Perumal drove ahead calmly. He went along sticking his head out the window and looking around. All the entryways, their doors locked, were silently getting drenched in the rain.

Right in front of them a little road would join the main road. At that crossroads, some cunning trap seemed to be lying in wait for them. Perumal put his head out in the pouring rain.

A big vehicle. Standing there trying to hide its monstrous body! . . . Perumal clenched his molars together . . . his face suddenly darkened and flushed.

Konamalai understood. His eyes reddened with a rush of blood. Then all of them understood. The insides of their skulls started buzzing. Their breath came fast and hard. Their bodies seemed to burn.

'Ready . . . Ready . . . Ready . . .' their hearts urged. They were prepared to receive orders. Their every limb began to quiver.

Konamalai seemed impatient.

'Come on, turn into that alley! We have to break through and get out of here . . . Where are they all positioned? . . . Have they surrounded us? . . . Damned rain!'

Perumal quickly began to back up. He looked behind him. From behind too, there was a vehicle coming at them like a demon!

Nearby a stream appeared, like an alley. Perumal made a huge effort to turn into it. But They had already overtaken them. Spouting fire, They began to close in steadily, fearfully, from both sides. The rain was blessing Them. The sky was looking at us with thunderclaps of laughter. Lightning was flashing, winking, as if to mock us.

Every second felt precious to them. Defeat came at them rapidly with its mouth agape. Are they to be defeated easily? Arul was in a great hurry . . . He shook his head this way and that. He trembled in the violence of his feelings . . . Do something . . . Quickly . . . Immediately . . .

Arul bit and pulled the clip in his mouth. Ayyo! Left hand . . . Left hand . . . It won't come, won't let itself be pulled out.

He could see clearly the horrible mistake taking place.

His thighs and ankles were strong as a horse's. Gathering all his strength in his toes, he sprang up. Hurtling momentarily through the demonically howling wind and the rain bearing down like great arrows, he fell into slushy rain-soaked mud. Swiftly rolling over four or five times, he moved away.

He'd understood . . . That's all . . . Just one more second . . . Arul! Oh, you idiot! You were in too much of a hurry!

His thighs must have been hurt. He got up limping. He started running wherever his legs took him. Rising rapidly up to his ankles, coloured with red earth, the flood water was rushing down through the alleyways. The alleys were giving way, unable to bear the slapping of his heavy footfalls.

Like a big thunderclap, the first explosion. The van jolted again. Continuing, one . . . two . . . three . . . four . . . five . . . six . . .

They stood still in fear!

Still running, he turned and looked back once. A great ring of smoke was rising up like a black ghost, shoving the rain aside. The suffocating stench of sulphur suddenly spread everywhere.

He ran without using his brain, his eyes staring straight ahead. His legs were dragging him swiftly, somewhere, all on their own.

Konamalai! . . . Perumal! . . . Kedari! . . . Periyannan! . . . Michael! . . . Anbarasan! . . .

That's it! . . . Now what? . . . That's it . . . They've been blown to pieces.

Now?

What should he do? Somehow or the other he had to get to the southern road safely. The stuff would come. He had to turn them in another direction. Had the men who were coming already heard the news and turned back? . . . Who could have told them? This wind and rain?

He had to get to the southern road. Damn you! Rain! Won't you stop? . . .

The sky gave a great clap of thunder for the last time and wore itself out. The rain began to subside. It showered drops on him like a sprinkling of rosewater.

He'd come running a long way. Maybe there was nothing to fear any more. He started walking with big strides. He still had three miles or so to go. He would get there . . . Somehow!

The rain stopped completely. An eerie silence set in. Trees that had been trembling with fear in the rain stopped trembling and shed tears. Only the flood came with him.

The alleys lay as if they were smothered in woven nets.

People were standing in the entryways of their houses. They stared at him. This strange, commanding young man, completely soaked in the rain, where was he off to in such a hurry!

He could rest a bit and then go on, stop to catch his breath and then go on! . . . Or what if he didn't go at all . . . What other strange things would they witness today!

Really, what if he didn't go at all?

People were looking at him strangely, eagerly, like a novelty. Was it some kind of fear that showed in their eyes . . . or devotion? Some people's eyes seemed to radiate unrestrained affection.

Faces appeared in the windows like moons. Pleading eyes bored into his face.

'Don't go . . . Don't go . . .' their gaze seemed to be begging.

If he liked, he could go into one of the houses and rest.

But he is not the one to go into any house! His task was the most important thing to him. He had to get to the southern road, and fast. He started walking on a road that split off from the alleys.

A few fields, eagerly lapping up the rainwater, watched him with silent gratitude as if he himself were the God of Rain.

He went on by.

A church appeared. The Virgin Mary, holding the baby Jesus in one hand, was looking at him tenderly. Lifting her other hand in the air, she sent him her blessings.

He kept going by.

A temple came along. Strange!

The temple was a little ways from the town. Chattering with palmyra tree fronds, with its doors wide open, it seemed like it was calling him. The temple tower, pointing to the sky, seemed to call out to him, 'Come.'

If he liked, he could go in the temple to lie down and rest for a while!

He would not rest. His task was the most important thing to him. He had to get to the southern road fast. Alone! Walking . . . or . . . running . . .

He started running again.

He felt a little exhausted. The shock, the running . . . He'd gotten a little exhausted, all right. If some van came along, he'd hitch a ride. He'd get there faster . . .

A little ways off he saw the path that joined the southern road, cutting across his path at a right angle. An old-time overloaded van was groaning along. If he clapped his hands, would they hear him? Would they stop? Would they take him along with them?

He clapped his hands. He clapped again and again.

'Can I come? . . . Can I come too? . . .'

He heard faintly as he ran:

'Come on . . . Come on . . . run! . . .,' A strange voice called out. It had an odd sound to it.

He was getting closer. There were a few people with bare chests. All men. Are they coming back from a temple somewhere?

He got very close.

The van stopped. New and unfamiliar faces! They were looking indifferently, off in random directions. No . . . No . . . No! Suddenly, they all turned towards him, as if commanded. Their eyes shone with hatred.

They all pounced at the same time. In their hands bayoneted rifles flashed. His heart stood still for a moment.

He was lost! He hadn't expected it . . . Even in a dream . . . That They would go around in such a disguise!

The guns closed in on him hungrily. A blow came down on his chest. Then a flawlessly aimed kick between his thighs!

He reeled and fell. Dragging him by the hair, they threw him into the van.

Bits of flesh emitting the nauseating smell of blood . . .

Konamalai! . . . Kedari! . . . Perumal! . . . Periyannan! . . . Michael! . . . Anbarasan! . . .

A borderless darkness surrounded him.

Translated by Rebecca Whittington

Ranjakumar, '*Kaalam Unakku Oru Paattu Ezhudum*' (1989), in Ranjakumar, *Mokavasal*, Yathartha, Paruthithurai, 1989, pp. 18–31

Woman Humiliated

Sivaramani

you cannot push me
behind the latticed window
of your definitions.
like a little pebble
plucked from where it's been
all this time,
lying in the endless mud
I
have picked myself out.

you cannot snatch
my days
between your fingers
closed over your eyes
like a baby star
bringing itself down
my being
has attained assurance.

I am she who cannot be disregarded.

what now
like a question that can't be cast off
I
am present
you cover me with insults
and uncivilized words

but,
I will sully
your shiny shoes
like a heap of dirt
on top of all your
civilized dreams.

as long as you reject
all my just words
there will be dirt
in your every path.

Translated by Rebecca Whittington

Sivaramani, '*Avamaana Paduthappattaval*' (1990), in *Sivaramani Kavithaigal*, Women's Study Circle, Batticaloa, 1993, p. 44–45

Darkness

Aswagosh

I lived
in the midst of white oozing wounds
the heart-rending cries
of decaying sons disturbed me
I was pained

I know
the faces of sons lost
long in the distance
I do not bother to ask
if in those faces
there was knowledge, beauty

I cannot disparage
the thoughts of sons
who knew only sacrifices
young sprouts
who caught a bus
hearts racing
and were swept up in the wind
I cannot throw out
yet another question

just yesterday
two died
I didn't ask for details

oh merciful one, did you hear
crows are cawing
a cock is crowing
trees are waving in the wind
deaths are taking place

the demon born today
ate up tomorrow's dreams
epic darkness descended

only time passed
there was no one to be seen
neither those who went far to pick fruits
nor those who showed the way
there was no answer to my feelings
seeking light

when I was still destroying myself
my son set out to find
a meaning for himself
to make his fortune

he went to lend his ear
to the voice of the earth
where my dreams are fallen.

it's not possible
for me to bear your absence, it's not possible
no
he is no longer with me
he went with an answer
to the voice of the earth

I will talk about memories
that trouble me
I will talk about the pain and heaviness
of those aching days of mine
in the language
spoken by oozing wounds
let me speak.

in the end
he came back to me
his body had gone cold
mosquitoes did not come to suck his blood
I did not let
the flies get close

Translated by Rebecca Whittington

Aswagosh, '*Irul*' (1990), in *Vanathin Azhaippu*, Nigari, Kalkilai, 1997, pp. 16–18

To Those Who Come with Sticks

Ilavalai Wijayendran

my
words alone have strength
not my body.

to scare the people
bring your concoctions of borrowed words
and pile them up.

shattering them
my words
stand upright

when you've lost to words
and come with sticks
to show your strength
what can I say?

Translated by Rebecca Whittington

Ilavalai Wijayendran, *'Thadi Kondu Tiribavargalukku'* (1990), in *Niramarru Pona Kanavugal*, Desiya Kalai Ilakkiya Peravai and South Vision, Colombo, Chennai, 1999, p. 56

Days in the Trenches

Pa. Ahilan

good friday
the day you were crucified
that day the burning wind
sweeping across sea and land,
a seagull or two
soaring in the spotless sky.
the sound of wind
scraping against palmyra trees
aroused an unutterable panic
that day was our last day in town
we came to the seashore.
only the waves returned.
when the sun fell into the sea,
we knelt down and cried.
a black howl arose
and night fell.
in the distance
like a corpse in the cremation ground
our town was burning.
good friday
the day you were crucified.

Translated by Rebecca Whittington

Pa. Ahilan, *'Pathungu Kuzhi Natkal'* (1992), in *Pathungu Kuzhi Natkal*, Kuruthu, Erode, 2000, p. 15

War Journey: Diary of a Tamil Tiger

Malaravan

The Battle Is On
15 November 1990

Around 5.10 a.m. the fog was still thick, and we parked the tractor, hidden in the tall bushes, and walked towards a hut to wash our faces. The darkness melted but the fog stayed on. On the left side of the road, set slightly farther back, there was another little hut.

'There's no point calling from outside the gate, let's go on in,' suggested Ranjan.

We removed the sticks blocking the gate's entrance and walked into the yard.

On both sides of the footpath, yellow and red flowers were in full bloom. The marigold flowers must have opened recently. The petals were moist and smooth. A large neem tree in the corner gave plenty of shade. A tiny shrine stood at the base of the tree.

'Amma, may we use your well to wash our faces?'

'Certainly, come on around here. There is some toothpaste out there too—go ahead and wash up,' the Amma said. Near the well the vegetable plot was lush and green. The vegetable plants struggled under the weight of their produce.

'How do you water these plants, Amma? Kerosene for the water pump is expensive, isn't it?' I asked.

'Who needs kerosene? We water with the *thula*. Our son helps. It takes maybe two hours.'

Her son, standing nearby, was only nine years old. I thought to myself that in Jaffna it is so very different. The children there would still be in bed or would have gone to tuition classes.

Today we depend so much on the food ships and trucks that bring foreign food to us. When will our own self-sufficient economy, destroyed by colonialism, sprout once again? Our economy will only grow when our people become aware of what has been done to us.

'Son, all of you, come on inside and have a cup of tea'.

'No, no, we'll drink it out here'.

'No, no, it's okay. Come on in and have your cup of tea'.

The cups were modest, but the tea itself, with fresh cow milk, tasted superb. We were all energized.

We said goodbye and went out to the road. We walked along the road and found a log to sit on. A monkey sat in a tree across the road and stared.

'Go stare at my grandpa,' said Master as he threw a stone at it. It jumped and ran off.

We ate the bread and plantains that Mani Annai brought, and discussed our need for sleep.

'Where will you be at noon?' Mani Annai asked.

'We'll eat and sleep here. We won't be going anywhere,' we said.

'I'm off, then. There are buns and biscuits in the tin'.

'Okay, Annai, see you.'

As soon as Mani Annai's head disappeared, everyone jumped for the bag.

'Leave it, boys. I'll distribute it,' said Master and he did.

The breeze was wonderful. We slept well. We tidied up the ground, removing the dead leaves, spread out some sacks and lay down. Shortly after noon we went for a walk through the paddy fields. We came to a mango orchard and a Lankan Government office with not a soul to be seen anywhere. We picked mangoes and sat down by a water canal to eat them. Two peacocks in the fields ran away when one of us stood up and shouted.

We started off at night and arrived at the Mankulam camp early in the morning. We kept quiet. From now on, it was of absolute importance that we maintain secrecy. Even if our own people saw us it was possible that the military could be alerted and our plans ruined. We strengthened the security lines around us. We stayed where we were until the next day, then we walked towards the camp to do some preparatory work.

16 November 1990

At 9.00 a.m. on the 16th morning, we arrived at our security posts. We sent Varman to his post on the other side of the camp.

'Master, look, let's stay in this house,' I said.

We went inside the house. I had seen this same house when I came here the first time, but now its outer walls were destroyed.

'Master, you're going to have to control the boys. They won't follow my orders,' I said.

'Just don't try and trick me again.'

'I promise,' I said and proceeded to put my hands on his head to gesture that this promise was real.

He stopped my hands, saying, 'Okay, okay, go on. I will control the boys. They'll never obey you because your face is too ugly.'

'Ok, I'll head on over to my post, then.'

I jumped over the barrier and stopped to chat with the other militants at their security posts, and returned to the house. Master and Alahu were tidying the house.

'Alahu, when did you get here?'

'This prince just arrived now. The idiot got onto the wrong tractor and went off to the other side of the camp.' Master laughed aloud. 'Hey! It was you who pushed me into the water, wasn't it?'

I read the situation quickly and realized I would be given a cold shower if I went up too close to him. I invited them into the house, but made sure to stand far away from them, and then I went and sat on the verandah.

Master called, 'Alahu, can you go inside and get the biscuits . . .'

Before he could finish, I rushed in to beat Alahu to the biscuits. When I opened the door, a bucket of water tied to the door tipped and drenched me.

Master's and Alahu's laughter was loud, and I heard it as I walked to the well with a defeated smile.

When we all lay down for a rest, Master asked me to tell him about Kannan, another Tamil Tiger warrior we knew—a militant—and how he died.

Kannan had been driving the tractor. He was sleepy and started dozing off. I kept tapping him to wake him up. He yelled at me for constantly tapping him. After a while, the tractor's course changed and it felt like we were going over a log. I couldn't see Kannan anywhere. I stopped the tractor, got off and saw that the log was actually Kannan. The tractor had climbed over his chest.

I fell asleep thinking about Kannan. He was a good weapon maker. He had joined the movement despite being the son of a big businessman and having the privilege that went with it.

22 November 1990

The 22nd arrived as we laughed, joked and worked. The morning was not that cold. The sun was up early too. Birds were busy singing and hopping around in the trees. Peacocks came down from the tree tops to the fields. They pecked at seeds on the ground.

Big flocks of parrots landed on the densely growing fruit creepers. Monkeys sat in the trees and watched us intently.

A gentle breeze embraced us all. Unwilling to leave the militants, the breeze banged its head on the walls of the security posts. Clouds rushed by after shedding a few tears and wiping their eyes. That sweet morning was bidding farewell to the militants. Birds sang mournfully and left. A rooster could be heard far away. We sat together for a cup of tea and began our preparations.

Master came and sat by me.

'What is it, Master? What is that look about?'

'I just wanted to have a good look at you before letting you go.'

'You bastard.' I started to chase him. We had lunch under the tree together.

The usual hot rays of the sun spread their calm heat on us. The *poovarasu* trees that droop in the heat were still standing upright. The breeze surrounded the militants and brought flower petals down from the poovarasu. The hut was cool and cosy. Even the crows crowed more pleasantly than usual, inviting their kin.

'If a crow crows while flying, a letter will arrive. If it crows while walking, a visitor will come,' said Master.

'What if it crows while it's sitting down?' I asked.

'Artillery shells will arrive,' he said.

We hurried to our meeting.

A large group of militants were sitting in rows. Their hands were firmly holding various types of weapons. Their faces were bright, alert and determined.

The female militants stood together on one side. They are the burning lights sprouting from a male-dominated society. They are making history.

A lieutenant in the front described the Mankulam camp thus:

'This camp was set up in 1971 to suppress an uprising among the Sinhala youth. It was re-established in 1978 and it remains a huge hurdle for our movement, a source of disruption in normal people's lives. It is a cruel camp and a threat to this whole area. We attacked it once before, but without success. We must make up for the shortcomings in that attack.'

Our discussion continued on to many more topics and was completed at 4.30 p.m. We returned to our posts and immersed ourselves in getting ready. Around 5.00 p.m. two Y-12 planes flew in from the south.

'Buddy, do you think he has been alerted?' asked Master, grabbing his weapons.

'Let's wait and see. They may be coming to drop off food,' I consoled him.

The two planes separated and started flying in big circles.

'Master, get the boys to transfer the shells into the bunker,' I said.

I watched him rush off. Ithayan was nearby, with his walkie-talkie in hand. Darwin was walking away with Master. Ranjan was squatting under a tree.

'Did he drop something?' Ranjan queried. 'Oh, he did!'

As all three of us watched, it came down with a hissing noise and hit the ground with a thud far away from the camp. Perhaps near the school.

'It's the "thing". This is all going wrong,' Master said, standing beside a nearby tree.

The other plane cut in and made a smaller circle.

'It's a bomb, look, it's coming down like a shuttlecock. All take cover!' As Ithayan said this, we could see it going past us and we froze.

Following the loud noise of the exploding bombs there was non-stop gunfire from the army camp.

'Do you think they've been alerted?' asked someone in a state of shock. As he said this a bullet hit a nearby tree.

'Is there a problem?' the leader asked through the walkie-talkie.

'No problem,' said another voice in the walkie-talkie.

Another plane circled round and round and dropped four parcels. One fell behind me. The next one was dropped in front of us just opposite the previous one.

'Buddy, this one is close to us, all take cover!' I shouted and everyone scrambled to take cover.

It came down with a loud hissing noise and exploded with a terrifying blast. The sand on one side of the bunker fell in from the shock.

We all came out brushing sand from our heads. The small hut where we were staying had disappeared without a trace. Near where it was, there was a huge hole in the earth. The planes had disappeared. We could now hear a howl of pain. We all walked towards it. The dog that we had been feeding for the last four days, less one leg and with a big wound, was lying on the ground.

'Master, look at our dog,' said Alahu.

'The poor fool. Now, now, don't start playing dog owner, go on and get to work.'

It looked at us pathetically.

'Okay, come on and bring all the shells out.'

The time was 6.05 p.m. The sun was turning red in the western sky. The sky, the clouds, and everything else was brushed with patches of red. Perhaps they were mourning the blood that was about to flow. Birds were hurrying back to their nests. Even the flapping of their wings seemed to presage sadness. Animals howled. Among all the sounds the howl of our dog gradually pervaded everywhere and everything and then eventually it died down, too.

A lonely lost heron flew past. Flocks of bats flew in patches. My heart was shaken by the sad songs of two lapwing birds that circled us, then the enemy camp, and then flew away. The sun was now buried in the earth. The clouds too had run away.

The time was 6.35 p.m.

'Buddy, is everything set up okay? Come over here. Shells and rounds will soon be flying and you're standing there without any cover. Be careful,' I warned those standing around.

The mouth of the cannon, camouflaged behind tree branches, was aimed at the police station.

The time was 6.56.

'Who's that?' I said sharply.

'It is me—Master,' came the reply. He took a pair of pliers and ran back.

The time was 6.58.

'Ranjan, is everything okay?' I wiped my face with the back of my hand. The walkie-talkie started and shone a red light.

It was 7.00.

'Okay, go,' the leader ordered and the firing noise of the projectiles shook the enemy camp before the guns there started to operate. The entire earth appeared to be shaking.

Noise from the camp was loud. It was the dying cry of the enemy. Enemy fire began to arrive everywhere. We faced the heaviest fire because we were very close to the enemy camp. Bullets hit tree trunks and branches, and exploded.

All types of bullets, some of them very powerful, were coming our way. Some of them passed between our legs. Yet, in this life or death battle, we sent a constant barrage of bullets their way and the confused enemy often fired in the wrong direction. Bullets went over the trees and even towards the sky.

'Look, from that post in the shop he's firing .30 calibre.'

We watched shells leaving that army post in all directions. The shop had caught fire from our attack. The ammunitions inside the shop had started to explode.

Every second, we received commands through the walkie-talkie about the modes and locations for our attack actions. We followed the orders. Gradually, the number of militants began to diminish as they were wounded and removed from the battleground. Those of us remaining continued with our attack. Suddenly, there were bullets coming straight down, hitting the trees. That was when we saw the two helicopters. They started firing into our positions.

Five-inch shells, RPG shells and many guns started firing towards us. We decided to take the plunge and attacked one target from three angles simultaneously. Our target, the police station, collapsed under our fire.

We would have suffered many more casualties if we had not adopted this strategy. Suddenly, there were two huge bangs and I felt my eardrums almost bursting. I felt blood oozing from my leg. It was a minor injury. Only later did I figure out that this was an aerial bombing raid by the enemy.

We continued with our fast attack when another bomber swooped down. Our .50 calibres were aimed at it and started to spit shells. The bomber rose up and backed away. Amidst the noise of the .50 calibre fire, we heard cries of pain. There was a problem at Cheran's post. I ordered the others to continue the attack and I ran to Cheran's post. Four young militants were lying in a pool of blood. Master also arrived from the next post.

'Take the boys away. He will hit again at that range.'

Carrying the young militants, we moved back. Soon the boom was heard again.

'Is there a problem, Master?'

'No, no . . . just a bruised hand. Walk fast.'

We had alerted the medics via walkie-talkie before we handed the four young militants over. The medical militants started first aid immediately. One of the four young militants, injured in the stomach, was lying in my arms. He grabbed my hand and tightened his grip. It felt as if he was using every bit of life left in him to tighten that grip. His voice too came out, using all the energy left in him.

'Buddy, invade the camp, kill them all, and grab every bit of equipment you can.'

His young life dissolved with the breeze and entered my heart and filled the space around.

His grip loosened. A star fell, leaving its silvery streak. The last words of the young militant echoed in my ears among all the outside noises. We hurried back to the battle ground. The bushes and the forest trees were burning, hit by shells and bombs. The shells and bombs continued to fall as we rushed back to our locations.

It was 10.15.

I briefed everyone about what had happened and readied the cannons. I began monitoring our target. Two shells from the enemy flew past us and exploded. Following an order from our leader, we aimed and our shell flew in the direction of the enemy.

'Buddy, it missed. Fire again before he comes out of the bunker.'

This time our shell hit the target and we could see the building crashing down. We sent an occasional 'light bomb' to identify our targets, and continued with our attack.

The next shell from the enemy hit a tree and Darwin's thighs began to bleed. I took out the cotton from the field compress in my pocket and applied a pressure bandage. The blood oozed through the bandage.

'It's okay, buddy. Set up the next one,' said Darwin.

'Are you crazy? You have shrapnel in your thigh. You can't stay here with blood pouring out like this.' I got mad, but he was adamant that he would stay.

The warmongers who are occupying our land are mercenaries working for wages. During battles, if their life is threatened, they hide somewhere and indiscriminately open fire. They back out of battle with the slightest injury. Our militants are very different. They dedicate their life and body to the battlefield. They value a free homeland more than their life. They never back away from a battle. They refuse to leave the battleground even if they are badly injured. They leave only as lifeless bodies or they are removed by others when they can't function any longer. This is the quality of our militants. It is this quality that paves the way for victories against the arrogant confidence of the occupier.

We continued with our attack. We had damaged their long-distance communication system, so one of their helicopters fired into their own camp. We stayed where we were, facing stiff attacks from the air and the enemy camp.

A plane began to circle overhead. We took cover immediately. A bomb fell just fifty metres away and a huge *paalai* tree (*Manilkara hexandra*) was broken to pieces; we were bruised by flying bits of the tree. Our attack came to an end when we took aim at the bank building.

11.59 p.m. The cannons boomed for the final time, shook the camp, and went quiet.

12 midnight. Their hands firmly holding their weapons, our militants started to crawl through the darkness. The night bid goodbye to them silently. Only the helicopters in the sky broke the darkness.

The grass gently stroked the crawling bodies. The grass bent over trying to make the path soft. There was no moonlight. The clouds hid the stars to keep the darkness as we crawled across the open paddy fields. With the enemy stunned by our fire, we crawled forward to destroy them completely and recover our land.

It was the enemy fire that started first, launching face-to-face fighting. The fire from the enemy camp intensified as our militants, sculptors of the future, crawled on with no cover. Finally, our guns began to show the enemy the truth. Enemy fire began falling in the open plain like raindrops. Helicopters, too, began their hunt for their prey in the paddy fields.

Helicopters were spitting .50 calibres non-stop. Our fire from the ground chased them back up to the clouds. Our brave militants began to float in a river of blood. Tiger soldiers jumped over enemy bodies to meet more of them. The enemy camp fell apart from our RPG fire and the mercenary force started to run away.

I turned the walkie-talkie on and our leaders' orders came non-stop. Jegan Annai and Vasthanan Annai were constantly being called over the walkie-talkie among the regular orders being issued. Then the walkie-talkie began calling for Thileepan Annai and Gopu. Their connection was broken. They were moving forward to capture the camp at the nun's hostel. I thought something must be wrong. It is very unusual for all the leaders of the four divisions moving towards a target to be cut off.

Yet, a little later, another voice said that they had captured some of the positions near that same hostel. Our leader congratulated them and promised to send reinforcements. I was able to work out that a battle was going on near the temple and our poralis were getting closer. Injured militants began to arrive from the division that approached the police station. I went behind them, along the railway track. Bullets were flying. I heard the groan of an injured militant. He was hit in the stomach and unable to move. I draped him over my shoulders and brought him with me. I could see bullets hitting the track in a line.

I sent my hands around the militant's neck looking for his cyanide capsule. It is the LTTE practice to remove the cyanide capsule from an injured militant's neck to prevent him from biting into it out of sheer pain. He grabbed my hand very tight.

'I am not going to die quickly without chasing away those bastards. If I can't today, I will come back tomorrow.'

He said this gritting his teeth in anger. He did not appear to be crying for the pain in his body. His thoughts were entirely on the battleground. 'Leave the rifle on safety,' he told me.

He fainted while he continued to grip my hands.

I changed the lever on the rifle and handed it to another militant, then I got out of there. Shells passed by me very close as I crouched and ran towards the gunfire of our division.

'Buddy, there is nobody who can carry those two over there, hurry up and take them in,' ordered another militant.

I slung the rifle back on my shoulder and moved, crouched towards the house that sheltered the enemy. Two militants lay there; they had lost a lot of blood. There was no bandaging material at hand. Where can one go to look for bandaging when shells are constantly whizzing past? I took off my Tiger striped shirt and cut it with a knife. I tied a bandage around the wounded stomach of one militant. His breathing was slowing down. The other had an apple-sized hole in his thigh. I wrapped that too.

I supported both militants on my shoulders and, hiding behind any available cover, I started moving back.

The one injured in the stomach kept trying to shout. 'Put one of us down and keep moving on inside.'

But his shouting came out soft in a pained voice. His hand folded over the rifle sling, making it impossible to remove it from him. His voice slowly got softer. I could now see a figure coming towards us.

'Hand one of them over to me, don't try to carry them both.'

'Master? I will carry both of them. You go to the front and bring someone else back.'

'Leo. Take them to the medics in the bunker near the tree.' I could see him running fast.

I handed over the two injured militants to the medics for treatment. As I turned to go, I could see medic-*poralis* in large numbers.

'No problem now. Bring any injured militant here immediately,' said one in the front as he ran, and the others followed him.

I waited near the tree for Master. The battle was intense.

I could work out from the messages over the walkie-talkie that the enemy was being weakened and that our divisions were entering enemy posts.

'Master, come. If we go to the post at the roadside, we can go down with the standby group. If not, we can at least go to the supply group.'

Both of us moved fast. Shells were exploding near us.

'We can capture half the camp today. Guarding the captured area from aerial bombardments will be very difficult,' Master said as he came towards me.

Translated by N. Malathy

Captain Malaravan, *Por Ula*, Publication Division, LTTE, Killinocchi, 1993; second edition, Vitiyal, Coimbatore, 2009

Extract from Malaravan, *War Journey, Diary of a Tamil Tiger*, translated by N. Malathy, Penguin Books India, New Delhi, 2013, pp. 59–73

A Space That No Longer Is

Su. Vilvarathinam

in the dawn
after the night all the village folk left
tearing life up by the roots
as the outsiders came in
the village
lies drained of the flood called life.

the whole sun
the whole moon
the whole wind,
the whole of the life of the courtyards
took its leave

the outsiders cut down the fences.
they broke down the front doors.
they plundered everything inside
the houses were left wide open

the wind blowing straight in through the open entryways
shutting, opening, shoving the doors
running inside, trying this one and that one
searching in vain for someone to relate to
runs through and through a space
that no longer is.

Translated by Rebecca Whittington

Su. Vilvarathinam, '*Vetraki Ninra Veli*' (1994), in *Uyirtthezhum Kaalathirkaga*, Vitiyal, Coimbatore, 2001, pp. 139–140

Heroes Rest Here

Cheran

in the terrible din of dried palm leaves breaking,
falling, swept up in the wind,
a koel
cries out in fear

to the west, a palmyra grove.

a flood channel running
with sand in the summer
and water in the winter

the south stretches ahead.

on the eastern border, Ponnipulam
a colony of landless people,
a colony of coloured people,
a colony of oppressed people.

red earth and fields to the north

and in the centre
stretched over the farmlands' disquiet
a burial ground,
a field of memorial stones.

the heroes' place of rest.

on this ground there are hundreds
sleeping.

those who walked
with upright chests
with vigour, with faces
shining with smiles
heartfelt friends,
relatives
and young men I don't know

for a moment my chest burns
the thoughts that rise in my chest burn
the story of life stretched out in thought
burns.

my people sleep here in this field
those who went too far to win
those who went up in the wind, in the sea
in the smoke
with them gone
they bring the leftover bodies
to bury them beneath the hero stones
and say it's your souls
that lie in all eight directions
from these stones.
Tamils don't believe the old story
that those who die heroic deaths
reach heaven
once a year
relatives, friends, and the 'state' too
will come round
to remember you

after mothers' tears
wash away the dust lying thick on the grave
in the long land of this graveyard
that grows memorial stones
they will shower flowers,
they will light a lamp and grieve;
wringing their hearts
they will sob out their stories of heroism

what did we remember?
what did we forget?

do not trust words completely
for within these heroes
dwell those who crushed
their enemies' military might
and also those
who chopped the heads and breasts of innocent people
night after night, wiping their blood-drenched faces
changing course changing tongue changing views
coming back victorious

this is the other side of heroism, sacrifice
all of these truths that live
in speech borne from ear to ear
honour does not lie only
in the thirst for destiny
do not trust words completely do not trust words

empty words embellishing your memory,
all the battle ballads
sung in every street
wither away by the fourth day

like the banana plants
that mark death in houses
and memory recedes
in the blood of children
caked on the sword of Cankilian
my dream disappears
in the wretched eyes of expecting women
destroyed by Raja Raja Chola
history commits suicide.
my poetry is drenched
in the sorrow of skeletons
buried under the Big Temple of Thanjavur

in history there are no heroes.
do not trust words completely.
in the sanctum sanctorum of time
I am waiting to tell the story
of a valour which will wash away the stain
I will sing then
of life, loss and death.

Translated by Rebecca Whittington

Cheran, '*Veerargal Thuyilum Nilam*' (1995), in *Sarinigar*, No. 172, (27 May–9 June) 1995, Colombo; published in *Vetraagi Ninra Veli*, Vitiyal, Coimbatore, 2001, pp. 15–17

One Night

Maalika

one night
I came out empty-handed
down into the street
with nothing
oh sun-god
roaming over my city
bring me the key I forgot to take
it must be under the thatch of the veranda
in the courtyard of the house I left behind
that is the key to my great-grandfather's strongbox,
ancestral land deeds
jewels for the body of Kaliamman,
my grandmother's
silver anklets,
bracelets, and the sword
with which she chased the devil away
in a trance
the brass lamp my mother lit
in her last days,
palm leaves inscribed with spells,
copper shields, images of cobras
and a few copper coins
I need these
to pass on to my
grandson tomorrow
so I can die saying, this is your land

these are your roots
oh sun-god, bring them to me.
I need my roots.
even though I will go tomorrow,
I need them today
bring them to me.

Translated by Rebecca Whittington

*Maalika**, '*Óriravil*' (1996), in *Erimalai*, September 1996; published in *Vetraagi Ninra Veli*, Vitiyal, Coimbatore, 2001, p. 47

* Maalika was reportedly one of the pen names used by the poet Pudhuvai Rathinadurai.

I Am a Snail . . .

Shanmugam Sivalingam

I am a snail
but can't freeze still
in the loneliness of this
disaster

among these ruins
how could I retreat
into my shell?

to the max I stretched and
stretched my feelers

I secrete slime
to slide across
these ruins
my slime freezes
in the rage of these ruins
I secrete even my colourless blood
and my flesh

I dig deeper and deeper
within myself to secrete
my heart
my intimacies
my feelings, even my
loneliness

within me
there is nothing
but the shell
an empty cave
I stretch my feelers
further out
to embrace my
ruined nation

Translated by Rebecca Whittington

Shanmugam Sivalingam, '*Sithaninthu Pona Desamum Thoornthu Pone Manakkugaiyum*' (1997), *Kalachuvadu*, Tamiliyal, Nagerkovil, 2010, pp. 195–196

The Eighth Ghost

V.I.S. Jayapalan

oh my neighbour, oh my neighbour
oh suns glowing in skullcaps and veils
oh moons playing joyfully on the sands
oh stars smiling in every cradle
our children have lost their way
they tore you apart
they wounded our Ealam soil
plaited with various flowers
that day we were silent
in your streets stuck with the
happiness of earlier days
and the blood-tears of the last day.
the next day we slunk in like foxes
and stole your very house.
we gulped down your children's food
we kindled our cooking fires with *meesan* wood
we tore apart your holy books
to wipe our spittle-covered hands.
that night that dawned without the prayer call
the angels disappeared waving their twelve arms
and seven ghosts followed.

among the seven ghosts that came following
the sixth pounced upon us
on those paths of your inconsolable
distress and tears

we too ran down
bearing harvested thorns

here comes the eighth ghost
before it rolls our heads
before it fills our princes'
coffins with earth
before it erases our poems
and writes lamentations in the wind
before it sweeps our poetic grandeur
into the dustbin of time . . .
we implore you . . .
oh my neighbour, oh my neighbour
come back and save us
with those six prayer calls
six times a day

Translated by Rebecca Whittington

V.I.S. Jayapalan, *'Ettavathu Pey'* (1997), in *Sarinigar*, No. 135, 20 November–3 December 1997, Colombo; published in *Vetraagi Ninra Veli*, Vitiyal, Coimbatore, 2001, pp. 41–42

(The background to the poem is the eviction of Tamil Muslims from the Northern Province by the LTTE in 1990.)

On the Surface of the Mind

Majeed

in the midst of the tender interstices of sorrows
that too came to pass—
by way of beautiful eyes
like a red-legged heron
from now on that too will settle on my shoulders.
there is nothing new to say
about what has happened
through the back door of its interior passage
through the seething force
of the lower surface of my mind
the potent force of my reality slipping
in the movements of fingers
in the strokes of eyelashes
in the rubbing of heels
spiralling up like a worm or
rising like the momentary smoke of burning trash
rainclouds of my trust and feelings crumbling,
truth and lies being, deep down, inseparably merged
of these
in the midst of the tender interstices of sorrows,
my mind will just go on singing to god.

Translated by Rebecca Whittington

Majeed, *'Ulmana Veli Parappinil'* (1998), in *Sarinigar*, No. 162 (24 December–14 January), 1998, Colombo; published in *Vetraaki Ninra Veli*, Vitiyal, Coimbatore, 2001, p. 25

The Sorrow within Me Has the Surface Area of a Straight Line

Majeed

two crying eyes
like deep chasms
echoed all your sorrows

my mind denies the sight
of the times held tight in a fist
like a butterfly with its colours smudged out.
to the small question time poses
so many replies have been uttered
wrongly.

the poem within me has the surface area of a straight line
what can i recite
for everyone to hear
time pierced me like a worm on a fish hook
and flung me into life

so many times I fell like rain
on the empty expanse of a desert
so many times I was dissolved
in the rain leaking into my hut.

like the ants' enchantingly ordered progression
I arranged the language of my heart
word by word in a straight line
a poem formed colourless

from now on, my mind will always deny the sight
of the times held tight in a fist
like a butterfly with its colours smudged out.

Translated by Rebecca Whittington

Majeed, '*Ner Kottu Parappalave Enakkullum Thuyar*' (1998), in *Sarinigar*, No. 152 (6–10 August), 1998, Colombo; published in *Vetraaki Ninra Veli*, Vitiyal, Coimbatore, 2001, p. 26

Lost Life

R. Muralisvaran

with an ascetic's
determination
the people
displaced in Vanni
again stood
asking for the boon of life

on this earth that had sprouted huts
a widowed mother
breathing darkness
lifted hands to jaws
and eyes to the sky.

the news—
they said
her son
lay buried in Semmani.
relatives—
someone said
lost money to the boatman
gave up life to the god of death
in the seas off Rameswaram.

why is she still
looking at the sky?

she could have looked at the earth
since that was where
she lost her son.
she could have looked at the sea
since that is where
relationships are lost.
so why did she look at the sky
was that where
she lost her life?

Translated by Rebecca Whittington

R. Muralisvaran, '*Tholaintha Vaazhvu*' (1998), in *Sarinigar*, No. 155, 17–30 September 1998, Colombo; published in *Vetraaki Ninra Veli*, Vitiyal, Coimbatore, 2001, 29–30

Veena

Bose Nilhale

in my time it never travelled with me.
even so
I lived with it.
when the veena floated in its own alluring sound
when I did not yet feel like an old man
when my skull was not burned by fear of the dark
when I was yet unable to feel
the cruel stench of war wafting
through the poems everyone wrote . . .
oh god!

the veena
in my time
never travelled with me
I lived in its sound.

yesterday
I felt like an old man
my nerves trembling with fear of the dark
in the poems I wrote in war-filled days
you can smell bones and hear the sounds of men and even nerves
oh god!
I have lost
even the last note of the veena that faded away in the wind

there was nothing in it but the waning moon
afterwards, every day
dawned by the sun
a poem long and dark.

Translated by Rebecca Whittington

Bose Nilhale, *'Veenai'* (1999), in *Sarinigar*, No. 172 (27 May–9 June), 1999, Colombo; published in *Vetraaki Ninra Veli*, Vitiyal, Coimbatore, 2001, p. 23

On the Present

Bose Nilhale

in the time that turns round
like a child crying pushing its eyes out
face shuddering
feet of dust climb on
at each time
self decays as time
tears and sighs and pining of men
wander as distinct faces
with their feet buried in dust deposits

the sky has lost its blue colour
and will no longer go on giving wings
to the angels

the beggar children stand
behind the smoke and dust and ashes
that reminds death
mocking time.
heading towards them
time turns at an even faster pace than
dust and ashes and smoke.
life dissolves
in the depths of their eyes.

Translated by Rebecca Whittington

Bose Nilhale, *'Nigazh'* (1999), in *Sarinigar*, No. 172, (27 May–9 June), 1999, Colombo; published in *Vetraagi Ninra Veli*, Vitiyal, Coimbatore, 2001, p. 22

Pyre

Rashmy

01.

black on red
or
red and yellow mixed half and half
a sprinkling of white
or
in the black border to a soft blue
designs and dots
dots and designs.

I was like a butterfly.

leaping and swimming in the wind
waving and waving my wings—the sky stretched out
without beginning in time

six legs smeared with pollen dust
impregnating the flowers
I wrote my poems in many colours

you eaters of boiled honey, what do you know
of the headiness of my honey and my languid song?

the moon
lost in the glow of my eyes
shards of a mirror shattered in anger
at being told it has lost its sheen
you yourselves call them stars
look closely at the mirror shards
I ask, do they not still glow
in the deep light of my eyes.
never mind, this is beyond your understanding.

I was like a butterfly.

02.

then this is what happened

that my wings should fade
and, turned to powder, should fly through the air
shedding their dots one by one—
so god cursed me.
he made a paste of neem leaves and smeared it on the flowers
not ambrosia but poison, he said.
he did an injustice.
time said,
two legs are enough for you
break the other four
and a pair of feelers
into kindling, to light the stove.

03.

what now?
the unappeased soul of a butterfly
now roams as a ghost, the townsfolk say.
the story spreads of a singing ghost
that comes out at night
children wet their beds in fear

with the swaying of banana and coconut leaves
and the fluttering of garments as they dry on the line
I come into being
mothers call on me to scare their children into eating.

04.

cruelty
it is cruel to turn from a butterfly
into a dead human.
even more cruel
to witness with human eyes
ants gnawing at the pyre
and dragging it away.

Translated by Rebecca Whittington

Rashmy, '*Eemam*' (1999), in *Kaavu Kollappatta Vaazhvu Mudalaaya Kavithaigal*, Exil, Coubevoie, 2002, pp. 49–51

The Song of an International Refugee

Shanmugam Sivalingam

I am a speck
but
a speck floating in the ocean

I am a wanderer
but
I wander
in a turbulent sea, a roaring
storm

I am a person with no refuge,
no, due to war i lost it, my
refuge

I am one
with many losses
but
not yet
to lose myself
in the war to recover what i lost

I am the grass trampled upon
but
a grass lucky enough
to witness a generation
which fights on

I am the one who runs
for my life, escaping missiles
and bombs
but
I have no history of
surrender

ruined, I am
but
not one without

hope.

Translated by Rebecca Whittington

Shanmugam Sivalingam, '*Oru Sarvadesa Agatiyin Paadal*' (1990),
in *Sithaninthu Pona Desamum Thoornthu Pona Manakkugaiyum*,
Kalachuvadu, Tamiliyal, Nagerkovil, 2010, pp. 205–206

The Echo of Moonlight

Su. Vilvarathinam

Parampu mountain.
Pari had died,
and the sun had vanished in the darkness.
Ankavai and Cankavai
were refugees.
They had fallen
to the 'royal drums beating victory'
and on their hill, on a narrow path
that seemed to be filled with the sorrow
of their downcast moonlike faces
Pari's daughters walked. Coming down
from the hill, the moonlight itself seemed to walk slowly
accompanying them like Kapilar, who had grown so old.

the moonlight,
Kapilar,
Pari's daughters
and the good life of Parampu.
They all walked
growing weary
weak and pale

With reverence Kapilar entrusted
Pari's daughters whose lives were broken
to Auvai and disappeared.
The journey continued.

Pari's daughters walked with Auvai
through all the villages
of the poor whose only food was gruel,
and the moon stood, hesitating, and went with them.

As if her long life
granted by Atiyaman's *nelli* fruit
were approaching its end,
Auvai hurried.
Sealing the marriages by pouring water,
she gave Pari's daughters
to the men who had destroyed their lives on Parampu mountain,
Pari's daughters who, like her,
made Tamil.
If only she had given them
to the families of men so poor
that, late in giving taxes,
they have only gruel or porridge to pay,
Pari's soul would have rejoiced.

That day, in the white light of that moon,
there was Parampu mountain,
and the drums beating victory,
and Ankavai and Cankavai
who became slaves in the harem of kings
and cried in pain—and now
on this day, in the white light of this moon,
their echoes still resound.

Translated by George L. Hart

Su. Vilvarathinam, *'Nilavin Ethiroli'* (1999), in *Uyirtthezhum Kaalathirkaga*, Vitiyal, Coimbatore, 2001, pp. 324–325

Inspired by the classical Tamil poem from *Purananuru*:

On that day, under the white light of that moon,
We had our father and no enemies had taken the hill,
On this day, under the white light of this moon, the kings,
Royal drums beating out the victory,
Have taken the hill. And we! We have no father.

THE SONG OF *PARI'S* DAUGHTERS, *PURANANURU 112*
TINAI: POTUVIYAL, TURAI: KAIYARUNILAI

George L. Hart and Hank Heifetz (eds), *The Purananuru: Four Hundred Songs of War and Wisdom, An Anthology of Poems from Classical Tamil*, Penguin Books India, New Delhi, 2002, p. 75

Anxious Sermon

Selvam Arulanantham

I left
and arrived on the thirty-third day
exhausted
as if I had been walking for ages.

the immigration official
was reddened
as if he were staring into fierce sunshine

born as a Dalit
bowed down as a Tamil
I felt myself black.

why have you come? he said
sir, I am one born
in a time when love has weakened
and atrocity has reared its head
I said.
I am one who lived
when stone turned into wood
wood into iron
and iron into fifty calibre.

staring at me again,
he asked, why have you come?

when he heard of my tragedy
of brothers fighting against each other
neighbours driving each other out
he asked, perturbed,
and what did you bring?
I said
there's a cross dragged across three thousand years
and the nails made over thirty.
he sent me into Canada with a handshake,
saying, you go nail yourself in
here,
where the flag with the leaf flutters
I will nail myself right onto the cross.

Translated by Rebecca Whittington

Selvam Arulanantham, '*Vyakula Prasangam*' (1999), in *Thotruthaan Povoma*, Sabalingam Nanbargal Vattam, Gorges Les Gonesse, France, 1999; published in *Vetraagi Ninra Veli*, Vitiyal, Coimbatore, 2001, p. 50

'Questions'

Aruntati

It was, indeed, an unexpected meeting today, and as the man relentlessly held on to me, I felt well and truly trapped. He looked like he was fifty or so, maybe even fifty-five or fifty-six. Evidently, he was a connoisseur of music. In a Tamil provision store. Now, I have this habit of singing to myself, just any old song that comes to mind. So I was standing in front of this pile of books, running my fingers across them, looking for this month's new issues, when he slowly came up behind me and asked, 'Little brother, you have a good voice. Do you ever sing on stage?'

I didn't know what to say. I wasn't even singing loud enough to be heard clearly. He could not have made out the lines of my song. Why praise me for singing well when I was only singing some random songs to myself?

Maybe he was teasing me. Who knows? That's probably why he asked me if I sang on stage. Or perhaps we share the same opinion about people who claim to be singers, but who really just pretend to sing.

What could I say? 'I wasn't singing anything,' I said.

'Come on, boy. What were you doing, then, just muttering to yourself?'

I'm done for! This man really means it. I don't even remember what I was singing, or if I sang it well. I just sing whatever comes into my head—a line here, a line there, whatever. It's a habit of mine.

It seemed to me that the man must be a good singer himself, or a connoisseur of music. His fingers drummed a beat on his thigh as he swayed his head and slowly hummed a tune.

I felt like laughing.

'Why are you laughing, little fella?' he asked.

I evaded the question. 'No, I think you have good taste in music.' I said.

'Well, why else would I drop what I was doing and talk about music with a complete stranger like you?'

Him saying he was giving up his work to talk to me was pretty amusing. In fact, here he was, talking to me, keeping me from getting my books so I couldn't leave and get on with my own life. How annoying!

'I rarely meet people like you, little brother. I'm not going to leave you.' He laughed as he said this, but I grew tense. I might as well forget my work for the day.

'Why, what do you see in me that makes you say something like that?' I asked. I was slightly elated, and rather eager to learn something nice about myself that I did not know.

'Tell me,' I asked.

'You really do have a good voice. You use it beautifully. And the books you choose to buy are not just any old books. You seem to be a good reader too. What else? I am, of course, happy to see people like this.'

That I read is true. But that I have a good voice or sing beautifully is doubtful. I felt like going home at once and really singing. In any case I could give it a try.

'Little brother, if you don't mind, I really want to talk to you. Why don't we go over there and have a cup of coffee?' he asked, almost dragging me along.

Now it all made sense to me. This was something I had done before, and now he was doing it to me.

When I was fifteen or sixteen, I and some other boys who were about my age or slightly older would go to festivals or folk performances. Whenever it happened to be folk theatre, it was really special. They would go on and on, until dawn broke. We mostly did not watch them from in front of the stage. We would much rather watch the 'other theatre' behind the stage. The wives of the performers would come and stand behind the stage with something heavy in the folds of their saris. It looked like it was really heavy. Initially we did not understand the secret of all this heaviness. The women would carry these weights and go behind the screen as though they had been instructed in what to do. At first we were not allowed in there, but then, little by little, we would help them carry this and that, and eventually we did get to backstage, close to where the screen was. That is how we learnt of the secret of the heavy things they were carrying. The performers in their costumes would make loud 'thom' 'thom' sounds as they jumped on stage, sweating as they sang. After a round of singing, they would come close to the screen and pull it so that the audience could not see their faces; then outstretched arms would give them one of the bottles that had been carefully guarded in the saris. They would gratefully gulp down the contents of the bottle, gently clear their throats, and enthusiastically return to conquer the stage, singing at a high pitch. After that it was sheer excitement! Ears would burst. The more of whatever it was their wives had kept hidden in their saris descended into them, the more joyous and exciting the performance got. Once we got used to all that, we regularly went back to watch the 'other theatre' behind the stage.

Performances in those days came with long stories. Like the Ramayana, the Mahabharata. The early King, the middle King and the late King—one King, played out by three actors. When the late King sang, the first two kings would be snoring backstage, asleep in their sparkling costumes. Half the people who came to watch the play would spread their mats, stretch themselves out, and dream about the climax. They would wake up with a jerk, rubbing their eyes as if someone poured water on their faces, when the late King was singing like a roaring lion. There were times when the performance would only end when the sun started shining on their faces, but the performers would mostly keep their costumes on the whole time. In their silk clothes and crowns they would light cigars or beedis, whichever they preferred, and go to a tea shop across the street. We would surround them, but the rest of the people in the town looked at them in amusement or just walked past them on their way to work. It was as if the actors were reluctant to step out of their characters. Maybe they were happy to be Kings and Ministers.

But their faces were horrible to watch. It was funny to see the pearl-white powder they had smeared on earlier in the evening dissolve in their sweat and peel off their faces. What was even funnier than this was to see the men who had put on female costumes. They would lift their saris and fold them up at their waists, remove their artificial hair buns and hold them in their hands while they lit their beedis or cigars. Their clothes would be crumpled, with one fake breast raised above the other sunken one. We tried hard to control our laughter. But we watched them seriously and enjoyed their performances. We kind of went crazy about them.

Sometimes this 'acting' was much better than their onstage acting. They would stand, sipping tea like kings. From the way they looked at us, they seemed to hope we would say something about the efforts they had put into their long night's performance.

I would go first. I would approach the one who looked the most anguished. 'Big brother, that was great! When you first raised your sceptre and pounded it on the ground and jumped up to sing . . . I just cannot forget that. It stays in my eyes!'

As I was saying this, the man would start loudly singing his song. The tea shop owner would clearly be trying to hold in his laughter.

We would each get hold of one actor and work on him, which would always lead to a re-enactment of the entire play in front of the tea shop. That's how our trick worked. Then, all in unison, they would order the tea shop owner to bring in milk tea for everyone. As if he had to be told. He was just waiting for this moment.

'Can I get you something else to eat?' he would ask as he served us some hot snacks, like a smart businessman. I have wondered since then if the old Tamil saying about raking someone to put on a show was actually said after our activities.

But now, beyond all my experience, this man in front of me was flattering me, just for a song that I was mumbling to myself.

Now we are heading over for a cup of coffee. There are a lot of Tamil restaurants in Le Chapel. It was rather a problem of choice. Instead of going to my usual place, I decided to take him to a different one. 'Ah, come in and sit down, brother!' the owner of the shop said affectionately, as though he had known me for years.

'I haven't seen you in a long time. Is it a holiday today?' he started questioning me. I normally don't like any of this banter. We might have met each other just the other day, but he would talk as though we were long-time friends, nearly placing his hand on my shoulder. He asked after me. I found it disgusting.

'What would you like to eat?' he asked.

I looked at the man.

'Just bring something that we can munch on,' he told him.

'And to drink?'

He said, 'Just bring us some coffee with milk.'

I don't know whose face I must have looked at when I woke up to make me so unfortunate today. The shop owner brought some coffee and snacks, and asked me, 'Brother, aren't you the one who writes poetry?'

That's it! Now this man who praised me for mumbling a song is not going to spare me at all today.

'I write a little. Have you read any of my poems?'

'Where do I have the time? But people who have read them say they are good,' he replied as he moved on to attend to the next table.

Businessmen are all the same, I thought to myself.

'Little brother, why didn't you tell me about this? When I saw your face I was right in thinking that you are very talented.'

The man acted like a scientist who had just discovered something new. Ayyo! Ayyo! What a pain! I felt like banging my head against the wall.

'I don't seriously write anything. I just scribble something now and then. Not much to talk about.'

'I have a real interest in all of this,' he said as he gave me a piece of paper on which he wrote something. 'Brother, my phone number and my name is on this paper. You really must come to my house one day,' he said. The name on the paper was Nallur Somasundaram. It seemed the man also had a taste for literature.

I figured that, maybe, talking to him wouldn't be a complete waste of time, after all, so I asked, 'Do you read books?'

He said, 'Yes, little brother, I read all the magazines and books that the boys bring me.'

'OK, but how about if we move on, then? I have some things I need to do.' I got up to leave and placed some money on the table for the coffee and snacks.

'Brother, why are you leaving? Wait, I've been talking with you all this time, and I don't even know your name. What is your name, little brother?' he asked as he held my hand. I said my name was Kanakalingam. He frowned and looked at me.

'Why, is there something wrong with my name?' I asked.

'No . . .' he hesitated and said, 'little brother, which part of Jaffna are you from?' he asked. I laughed.

'You laugh at everything. Just tell me where you come from,' he said.

'Why do you think I am from Jaffna? Not from Batticaloa or Trinko. Could even be Manar, right?'

'Can't you tell where a person comes from by the way he speaks?'

I guess he thought this was an important contribution to linguistics.

'If that's so let's see if you can tell me where I'm from?'

'It could be guessed . . .' he hesitated and then after a moment, he said, 'Here everyone's the same. This is all the work of those crazy Europeans. They give a card and a job to everybody who comes here, and now they assume we're all the same.'

What is he talking about? Oh, is he trying to tell me that there is so much violence and murder here because the Europeans have allowed the coexistence of both those who carry arms and those who work for peace? But what is the connection between this and that talk about where a person comes from?

'Little brother, go on. You said you write. Do you have a job?'

Perfect. Whether the man knows literature or not, he indeed knows about writers. But even then, I thought he should not have asked me that question after eating the snacks and drinking the coffee that I just paid for with my own money.

'I have an eight-hour cleaning job.'

'You see? One has to come all the way here to be a janitor. Everything is upside down here. What were you doing back in Sri Lanka?'

'I was studying. Where did I study? I spent all my time watching theatre.'

'I never miss listening to plays on the radio, but I don't watch plays performed on stage,' he said.

'Why not?' I asked.

'Don't you know about the people who stage these plays there?' he asked with a smirk.

I thought the man was morally outraged about the third-rate cinema-style plays of his own time, and asked, 'Wasn't there the great actor Vairamuthu in those days? There was no one then who could outperform him in singing and acting,' I said.

He laughed strangely. Then he said, 'It seems my little brother hasn't properly understood what I meant. Everyone should do what they are meant to do. Didn't they too go around with guns, claiming to fight for liberation? Did we allow them . . .?'

I got it. I understood everything, just when I was about to make my getaway.

'Little brother, you look like one of our boys. You still haven't told me about your native place?'

I told him. He shot me the next question. 'Oh there! But which area there? By the side of the temple or behind the temple?'

I told him.

'Then is it on this side of the junction or the other side?'

I told him that too.

'Then is it by the side of the field or by the side of the pond?'

I told him.

'What's your father's name? What does he do?'

After a moment of silence, I said, 'Why are you pestering me? What you are thinking is true. I'm not one of your boys.'

He stood up in a hurry.

'Little brother, I just remembered something. I have to go.' He turned to look at me.

'Like I said, little brother, I just remembered something. We are moving tomorrow. The telephone number I gave you just now will not work. I'll look you up later and give you the new number,' he said as he left.

This is all the work of those crazy Europeans: I just repeated, inside myself, what he had said earlier.

Translated by Kiran Keshavamurthy

Aruntati, *'Kelvigal'* (1999); first appeared *in Uyir Nizhal* Journal, Paris, March–April 1999; published in Sugan (ed.), *Theendathagaathavan Muthalaana Eelathu Dalit Sirukathaigal 14*, Maalika Books, Chennai, 2007, pp. 128–141

Earthen Towns

Nilanthan

JAFFNA, OR THE CITY OF PEACE

(A few letters that came from Jaffna after people returned home in April 1996)

this year, a very long summer
nothing but sunshine,
wind moving mysteriously like a spy.
night
belongs to howling dogs
and growling trucks
daylight is
the time between
two curfews
the street stands broken up between one checkpost
and yet another checkpost
life is a barren dream
surrounded.

(24/6/1996)

SONG OF RETURN TO THE CITY

(to be sung to the Catholic folk theatre tune '*Melinjimunai*')

ask the sun that burns dry
every one of our streets
ask the wind that speaks
with our stiff palm trees . . .
ask the sun . . .

our village is burned
our houses alone
our wind breathing death
our hearts have been charred . . .
ask the sun . . .

in our town's rotting mouth
we can see from far away
palm trees sprung from our land
are calling us home . . .
in our town's . . .

our sea our fields
our land our lake
our plains our woods
our river our people
are ours, are ours
are ours, are ours . . .
ask the sun . . .

- Written on 21.11.2001, The Day of the Suran War, Tirunagar-Mallavi
(Suran War refers to a popular festival that celebrates the killing of the demon Suran by Lord Murugan.)

EARTHEN TOWNS

yesterday
the day after Killinocchi fell
we went to Mullaittivu
instead of Yappu Pattuna
Mullaittivu
instead of Mullaittivu
Killinocchi

instead of one town
another town
towns on top of towns
big towns and little towns
all towns laid waste

unconquered people
are either killed or
flee to the forests
at times
they return victorious
and then
in place of the old demolished town
they build a new town
with earth

the whole of Mullaittivu laid waste
what men built
men demolished
men killed men
and burned men

but ever older and bigger than men
is the sea
unharmed by anything
beyond all lack of certainty
as a single certainty
it's like an angel
the beautiful sea,
like a sage
at peace,
coloured like all the blue of the sky
dissolved and turned into the sea
men come and men go
cities are built and ruined
but the sea
neither comes nor goes
in war or in peace
nothing can touch it

look
the men are coming again
now
they will build a town of earth

oh . . . sea,
old sea,
oh dear, great sea,
keep in touch with the earthen towns

they conquered
a great ocean
but they lost
another capital.

the other day, Killinocchi fell,
when they entered the town
to aim the gaping cannons
bursting open its little streets
full of jostling people,
only a dog was left behind

unconquered people ran
and hid in the forest
calling the birds and all the other
grateful animals
there they would build
a town of earth.

that earthen town
just like their
trenches
will be dark
and beyond time
just like their beliefs
about the future
it will be easily demolished
before the cannons' insatiable hunger
without protest

oh . . . forest
old forest
oh dear, great forest
be the consolation of these earthen cities

over the fields of screeching lapwings,
they wander without support,

these earthen cities
are drenched in rain,
the rain chases them
like a ghost
when on one accursed night
they left
their capital and ran
the rain
was chasing them
just like this
just like the enemy.

forest
oh good forest
don't let them down

sea
oh good sea
don't let them down

rain
cruel rain
oppresses my people
my innocent people
are delirious
with sorrow
like widows
who have lost their youth
on sloping roofs of earthen towns
endlessly getting soaked in the rain . . .

oh . . . capitals
with spacious grounds
oh marketplaces
full of valour and joy

oh grand
famous avenues
beloved palmyra trees
listen to me . . .

Translated by Rebecca Whittington

Extracts from two long poems '*Vannimaanmiyam*' and '*Yaazhppaaname, Enathu Yaazhppaaname*!' by Nilanthan; *Vannimaanmiyam* first appeared in *Niyathi*, Mallaavi, 2002. '*Yaazhppaaname, Enathu Yaazhppaaname*!' first appeared in *Magizh*, Puthu Kudiyuruppu, 2002. These poems are published in Nilanthan, *Ini Enathu Naatkale Varum*, Vitiyal, Coimbatore, 2012.

Hanifa and the Two Bulls

Kumarmurthy

Vellayan mustered all his energy and let out a high-pitched bellow, almost tearing his vocal chords in the process. Completely rattled by the sound, Hanifa ran over to look. Vellayan lay stretched out in the shed, his pained eyes rolling in and out, lit by the faint moonlight. His hind legs twitched in rapid convulsions. Startled, Hanifa circled around randomly. He had no clue. He ran back to the house and brought out a tiny lantern, burning like a firefly. He kindled it and it crackled and came to life, with a brightness that strained the eyes. He held the lantern up and checked again. Vellayan was in the same state. There was complete silence all around. Suttiyan was glaring right through the night, with his ears all erect. Hanifa sat down next to Vellayan and caressed his chin. Tried to lift his head up, in vain. He shouted towards the house, where he could see his wife coming out the front door.

Together they tried to get Vellayan to stand up. Somehow, Vellayan managed to squat like a 'Nandi', frothing around his mouth. Hanifa trembled looking at him. Tears welled up in his eyes. He tried his best to recount the day, in sequence. Nothing unusual had occurred. They had been working for the whole week in Maniyam's paddy fields. All the tilling and turning over was done by Vellayan and Suttiyan. It's been so for years. Once Hanifa steps into a field, Maniyam would never even bother to look in that direction. All he had to do was relax, sending everything, from betel leaves to chew on to seeds for planting, through his workers. Or he would attend to other jobs in hand. Hanifa's work was impeccable. He never bothered about time, as if he was working for himself. He wouldn't want to go anywhere else until he completed Maniyam's job. He had finished it all up now, but for a single day's work.

While he worried about the sudden sickness of Vellayan, he was equally disturbed about leaving Maniyam's job unfinished. He asked for some salt to be mixed in warm water and sat next to Vellayan. Feeling a little sense of relief, he hugged Vellayan once, who nodded in appreciation despite being exhausted.

Vellayan had known Hanifa ever since he was born. Hanifa was everything. An unimaginable sense of gratitude hence stayed with him perpetually. His mother died soon after his birth. Orphaned and famished by the time Vellayan managed to reach Hanifa's hands, he didn't look like he would survive for two more days. Hanifa looked after him like a son. Even his wife complained a bit. But he nursed him back to life. Vellayan would run around the house, playing with the kids. His character never changed, even after growing into a bull. He would often just stand there with those longing eyes of his, waiting for somebody to bring in his fodder. If that someone's hands were empty, Vellayan would come after them, playfully. He would never wander very far, even when he was outside. The moment he heard the call, 'Vellayan', he would come running. His name, 'Vellayan', means milky white, which was his colour. Not a single spot on his body. When he was scrubbed clean with soap, he would gleam as white as a nettle flower.

But Suttiyan was found by chance. Hanifa immediately realized that he would make a good team with Vellayan. It was not easy for him to buy Suttiyan. Hanifa was not well to do, living as he did on his daily wages, but it was not a difficult life either. He got work for thirty days of the month and gained a reputation as a good farmhand. He was well built and tall. His hair was just about to turn grey. He chewed betel leaves all the time, filling his mouth. He never missed the morning prayer in the mosque. Moreover, he also participated in the administration of the mosque. Not just him, this had been the case for generations. It had become a fact of life, beyond any need for explanation. It had nothing to do with the concept that performing your duties would help fulfil the lives of your children. It just happened that way.

He gently put the soda bottle filled with salt water into Vellayan's mouth, holding his chin up. Vellayan gulped all of it quickly. This gave Hanifa a certain confidence and peace of heart. He asked his wife to make some tea, and leaned back against the pillar, next to Vellayan.

Hanifa was as affectionate towards Vellayan as he would be to any of his own siblings. This was reflected in every word he used. He would never hit him. If Hanifa simply raised his voice in anger, Vellayan would recognize it and act accordingly. Shaking the bell around his neck once, he would quicken his pace. But Suttiyan would, occasionally, get hit: he had a stubborn streak. When they finished work, Hanifa would take bath only after he washed them both up. Suttiyan would run to the house, but Vellayan would wait for Hanifa and walk home with him. Sometimes on the way home, Hanifa might chatter a bit longer than usual at the shop where he bought his betel, and Vellayan would gently nudge him on his backside to remind him. Hanifa would excuse himself, saying, 'He is hungry,' and leave.

Once, about five years ago, it was drizzling, a cold breeze was blowing and the sky was loaded with dark clouds and lightning. Hanifa tied the bulls in the shed, arranged hay for the night and went to bed. At midnight, awakened by Vellayan's cry, he came out to look. The wind was heavy, and the coconut trees were dancing around like devils. The rain got heavier. Vellayan jerked and cried out again, four or five times, heaving in anger. In this ruckus, Hanifa's wife and children also came out of the house. A few minutes later a coconut tree broke and fell headlong on top of the house. Amazed, everybody hugged Vellayan in gratitude.

Sitting there, Hanifa looked up at the sky. The moon was visible, hazily though, hidden among the clouds. Hanifa tried to remember that day's crescent, but his memory refused to help. He assumed that it would be just a little while before dawn broke. At that moment he heard, outside, the inauspicious crowing of the cock. A dog howled in the distance too, then it faded out. Hanifa was a bit rattled, wondering what evil was going to strike. He thought for a moment about his son, working in the city. He had written saying that the army would shoot people at random. He prayed, strongly, for nothing of that kind to happen. Muttering 'inshallah', he looked in the direction of the mosque but he couldn't see it right then.

His wife brought out the tea. He drank it down and then they both tried to lift Vellayan again. Exhausted, Vellayan squatted like a Nandi again, breathing noisily, struggling. Hanifa used his hands to wipe the froth from Vellayan's nose. His hands got sticky, and he wiped them on his shoulder towel.

His worries doubled when he thought about Kaja Moideen's absence. He was an expert cattle healer, and he always responded promptly to any call. The entire village had been shocked when they brought him home dead, killed by a bomb.

As daylight fell over the earth, Hanifa handed Vellayan over to his wife and hurried off to find Maraikkayar. Maraikkayar was shaken when he heard Hanifa speak. He had never heard Hanifa's voice trembling so much.

'What is it, Uncle?' asked Maraikkayar, rushing out of his house. Listening to Hanifa, Maraikkayar said, with raised eyebrows, 'He wandered by here last evening and seemed fine then.' He turned back and called for Hussein. Hussein came out immediately, as he was preparing for his namaz.

The three of them tried together to get Vellayan up on his feet. But he could not get up, and slid back down to the ground. Then somehow they succeeded in stretching out his legs and he stood up, trembling. They examined his body thoroughly, not leaving a spot unchecked. Nothing seemed to be wrong. Maraikkayar felt the chin, the front legs and eyes, for a second time. They seemed a bit swollen. Nodding his head in pride at having diagnosed the problem, he said it must be '*mun adaippan**'. The other two, after second examinations, agreed with him.

'Doing "*naiyyam*†" twice will make it vanish. Put the burden on Allah! All will be fine,' said Maraikkayar. Hanifa looked up to him in hope.

Hanifa took a deep breath and looked at the sky. They let Vellayan lie down and started discussing the logistics of 'naiyyam'. Suttiyan, standing next to Vellayan, was licking him.

The village seemed to be in a rush. People were hustling and talking, in worry and surprise. The afternoon sun was blinding.

Exhausted, Hanifa wiped his sweat off with his towel. He was carrying palm flowers and neem seeds, collected for 'naiyyam' over some four or five miles. His mind was preoccupied with Vellayan's recovery, plus he was constantly mulling over plans to finish Maniyam's job, with an alternative pair of cattle, if need be.

When he entered the fence gate at his house, his wife and children were standing at the front door. Their faces were shrunk and darkened in incredulous sadness. Hanifa's head reeled when he saw them. Thinking that something had gone wrong with Vellayan, he rushed to check and found him lying on his side, on the ground. He checked his breath, and found it coming, irregularly. His youngest daughter came and stood behind him.

'Father, we all have to leave,' she blurted out.

'Listen to your mother, my child,' said Hanifa, opening up his sack, hurriedly laying out his bundle.

---

* A disease that affects cattle, arresting their ability to masticate.

† Mixture of neem seeds and palm flowers.

But his wife also hurried over to them, and wailed, 'The Movement has asked all of us to leave . . . Oh Allah, how unfair is this . . .' That's when it struck home to Hanifa, and he remembered Vellayan's cries. His mind finally absorbed the fact that something else, something thoroughly horrible, was really happening.

He walked up to the road in a daze, and saw faces shrunken, inexpressibly sad. He saw lots of people heading to the mosque, and children scrambling all around, raising dust on the street.

Two vehicles, one after the other, went past him, with guns protruding out of them. When he saw that Maniyam's younger son was in one of the vehicles, out of habit he started to call out. But for some reason, he could not. It seemed as if something came and blocked his throat.

When the dust settled, he sensed Maraikkayar's presence next to him.

'What's happening, Uncle?'

'We have to get out of the village.'

'Where to?'

'Only Allah knows,' said Maraikkayar, pointing to the mosque and walking away.

His brain was not so clear, but instinct told him that something terribly wrong was happening and he started walking back home. He went up close to Vellayan and looked at him. His eyes were closed, and his ears were quivering. Suttiyan was standing next to him, still busy licking.

He felt the urge to howl with all his strength. He just sat down, dizzy. Something heavy was rolling up from his stomach, grabbing his chest. Thoughts went numb. His ears could hear familiar voices, wailing and whining. He shut his ears too.

His youngest daughter pulled him, saying, 'Everybody is leaving, come on, Vaapaa.' Hanifa stood up and followed her in a daze. His wife and elder daughter were walking ahead, carrying a small sack of clothes. When something hit his backside, he turned around to look. There stood Suttiyan. Hanifa lost all control and burst out wailing non-stop, and hugging his neck. People in the street watched as they walked past in single-file lines. His younger daughter pulled him away, to walk with her. Suttiyan came along as far as the gate. When they turned into the street, Suttiyan turned back to look at Vellayan. Then he looked again at them.

As long as Hanifa could see him, Suttiyan kept taking turns, looking at them, then at Vellayan, then back again.

Translated by D. Senthil Babu

Kumarmurthy, *'Hanifavum Irandu Erudugalum'*, in *Kumarmurthy Kathaigal*, Kaalam, Toronto, 2002, pp. 29–35

(This short story recollects events around the LTTE's chasing out of Muslims from the Northern Province of Sri Lanka in October 1990.)

A Story Lost in Time, Lasting in Time

Iravi Arunasalam

I remember those days. Even though I was already thirteen years old, I still held my father's hand when we went anywhere.

It was 1974, in the month of *Thai**. Those were happy times. Before this story, which I am about to relate, there came these heavy monsoon rains. Fields flooded. Backyards were brimming with mud. Wary of stepping on snakes in the floodwaters, we went into nearby fields and collected tapioca tubers. We picked brinjals. Floods don't hurt bananas, but so what? Vasanthan went ahead and bagged them too.

Because of the floods, there was a bumper crop that season. I wish I could say that was a time of overflowing, exuberant rivers. But we had no river in our town. Just a canal that we called Vazhukkai River. It ran when the monsoon rains poured down. The rest of the time it was just sand that ran there. We ran there too. Wells all over town were overflowing. Our hearts, too, were overflowing with joy. Torrential monsoons meant cold, dewy winter mornings that would keep us wrapped up in blankets.

Then came the days when we could no longer stay wrapped up in our blankets. We were so happy! All the streets were festooned with banana trees, and shrines were built at every street corner. Banners beckoned in front of all the shops. Full pots sat waiting, along with strings of auspicious mango leaves, at every doorway, in every household.

* Mid-January to mid-February.

What for? For a carnival! For whom? For us, for our mother tongue, a festival was happening for our Tamil language! We were ecstatic.

Sound the conch!
Our life, our wealth,
Our Tamil will never grow dim!
If anything comes to threaten it
Destruction is certain so
Sound the conch!
Hold your head high, and
Call yourself a Tamil, man!

Such were the words chiselled in our hearts, at that tender age. Naturally, we were happy about the festival. Cold in the morning, cold in the evening, but the days were sunny. Buds started to ripen on the branches of the jujube trees. We explored the whole town looking in vain for one single ripe berry. We didn't notice the time flying by; it was just filled with happiness. Why would we hold back when there is a festival for Tamil?

In 1968, Chennai, the capital of Tamil Nadu, had hosted a Tamil Research Conference. Scenes from that conference were shown as trailers along with the movie *Ooty Varai Uravu*, starring Sivaji Ganesan. That's why we went to see *Ooty Varai Uravu* at the Mani Mahal Theatre in Sangani. That's how avid we were. And now, how could we sit still when such a festival was taking place in our very own country? I dragged my father along. Mother said she wouldn't come. My sister, I and Siva held father's hand as we went. We watched the festival. We were ecstatic.

That's how I remember it. Not a single moment forgotten. Our hearts were overflowing with Tamil. Somehow, even now this is how it seems to me. That was the moment when Tamil touched our very hearts. Before that Tamil was a language. It was *just* a language. After that, Tamil became our identity. It became our consciousness, and mixed, as one, with our lives. We all joined together, in determination, as Tamilians. Those were the days when I went to the Tamil Research Conference, holding on to my father's hand.

There was a parade. The floats featured all kinds of figurines, tableaux and skits, all celebrating the glories of Tamil. We watched it from the corner of Kasthuri Street, then we ran to the corner by the Windsor Theatre and watched it some more. But that was still not enough. Some people told us there was another parade over at the end of Paramesvara Street, so we ran over there and watched that too. We were in seventh heaven.

I got this feeling in my legs. That's how I remember it. They started to tremble. I tried to plant my feet firmly on the ground. Normally, I let my feelings show. I cry, not out of grief, not even in times of soul-wrenching misery. But at that moment I was about to cry. But nothing much happened. My legs started to tremble and I planted my feet squarely on the ground.

But no, my consciousness won out, or at least that's what I would like to say happened. Now my legs stopped trembling and I rooted my feet to the ground.

Oh, man, how can I express that feeling? I don't have the words. Father's hand, holding mine, was firm. Father sent me a message through his hand, and I, in turn, sent the message through my legs into this earth, my Motherland. But I cannot, now, seem to explain that feeling.

In the swirl of all those emotions, we arrived at our house, lit by a kerosene lantern. In the courtyard, with a cool breeze blowing, we told mother all about the day's events.

I pestered my father all through the next day. I pressured him. 'We have to go on the final day too!' I said. I knew the last day would be the pinnacle of the festival. I would not leave my father alone. 'Okay,' he said, and so father and I went.

That evening we were standing on the streets in Jaffna town. There were banana stalks, banners, shrines and figurines everywhere. Bamboo and casuarina poles were erected, and coloured lights were hanging from them, blinking lights. It was all just beautiful. A chilly breeze was blowing, but I was happy.

I repeat: Everyone was happy. Not just happy, though. Everyone was emotional.

I could see it clearly. Each person's face shining in the lamplight. We're gathering in front of the Regal Theatre, and walking from there to Veerasingam Hall. We're standing in the open square. A rally is taking place. I couldn't see. I was a kid. Short of height, I couldn't see anyone. My toe tips hurt, I was straining so hard to see. My father wasn't going to pick me up. The loudspeakers were the only things that helped me. There's a noise coming from the loudspeakers.

No. The more I think about it, the more it seems like the loudspeakers were switched off. No, I can't be sure. Were there loudspeakers or not? Whatever, there were some jumbled, confusing words coming at me. I can be sure of that much. My own emotions were rising, and I could feel the sweat on the palm of my father's hand.

There was a police station by the pannaikkadal. The sea breeze from pannaikkadal came spreading through the entire town, as if it were bringing some news.

This is all I can manage to say now. What happened next? Something that made us wonder what crime we had committed, besides speaking Tamil. We did put on a festival for Tamil, but that's all. But because of that came something crazy, unreasonable.

The lights went out. Wires fell from the electricity poles. That's all I could see. Sparks arced and fireballs flew. Father clutched my hand and hollered my name, 'Raasa! Raasa!' He dragged me along, running. I heard gunshots. Gunshot sounds that I heard once in a blue moon, when somebody went hunting in our village, or when they shot a mad dog, I now heard continuously. The hunters have come. Or maybe it's the people who shoot mad dogs who have arrived.

Bombs fall, exploding white. Eyes burn, but regular smoke doesn't make them burn like this. It was like the smoke when they burn rubbish piles in the village. It burnt when I was asked to spit on burning chillies and neem leaves to placate the evil eye, but it had never burned like this. This, this *really* burned.

Eyes burning more and more, father keeps on running, yanking me along. I stumble along, running with his pulling. Where are we running to? No idea. I pulled on my father, and he pulls me, and he runs.

Suddenly, father falls into a ditch. And when he falls like that, how can I keep from falling too? I fell. Head first. That's my memory. Face smeared with mud.

Like I already said, it was a good monsoon that year, and it smeared its mud all over me, uninhibited. It probably smeared my father too. I wasn't sure, though, in the dark. We just stayed there, in the mud.

More and more people keep falling into the same ditch. From the way they were falling we can tell it's not really a ditch. It's a storm sewer. We are lying in a storm sewer. Father keeps whispering, 'Raasa! Raasa!' as he rubs my back. He doesn't say anything else. He didn't ask, 'Are you hungry?' If he had, I would not have said yes. He didn't ask, 'Are you scared?' If he had, I would not have said yes.

This is all my father did.

He rubs my back. In the dark, his hands move from my back to my throat and feel around my face for my eyes. My father's fingers.

'Father, I am not crying,' I whisper.

'Doesn't it hurt?' he asks

'Yes, Father,' I said.

'Everything hurts,' I said.

I think my father then whimpered, 'Raasa!'

Dawn broke and light returned. Father arranged some stones and climbed out, then he pulled me out as well.

We went to the bus station, but by a circuitous route.

There was no bus. Father said, 'Let's walk.' We walked ten miles to get home. We passed ponds, fields, and temples. Reached home. Landing on our doorstep, my mother shrieked when she saw how I looked.

That was the day our whole town, our whole nation, began to shriek.

Translated by D. Senthil Babu

Iravi Arunasalam, '*Kaalam Aki Vanta Katai*', in *Kaalam Aki Vanta Katai*, Vitiyal, Coimbatore, 2003, pp. 21–25

(This story is set against the background of the violent events at the World Tamil Research Conference held in Jaffna, in 1974. The massacre took place on the last day, 10th January.)

Questions for the One Who Is Coming

Karunakaran

what is this constant obsession of yours
with this race
in which we will never meet
in those mysterious moments of your arrival
raking up dust choking the sky
sounds of horse hooves
through our courtyards
when you come
breaking down
in fear
we run away
carrying ourselves like corpses

in that last moment
the remnants of our life lay weeping
on the cornerstone of a house reduced to dust
the garden laid waste.
you have seen
our happiness littered
among the ruins of flowering trees.
all the times you came that way
only sorrow was in the making.
doesn't it bore you
being set to follow

love's yarn breaking
the invariable gap of impossible meeting?

don't you ever want
to stretch out a hand of friendship
under that ray of light?

Translated by Rebecca Whittington

Karunakaran, '*Varugaialaridam Sila Kelvi*', in *Oru Payaniyin Nigazhkala Kurippugal*, Magizh, Putu Kudiyuruppu, 2003, p. 36

Appe Ratta!*

V. Gowribalan

He isn't a mythical being, something you cannot easily see with the naked eye, yet you would never come across him in the normal, mechanical ruckus of your life and work. When he is not out picking up scrap iron, which he does in order to feed his belly, he'll stand rooted, intensely gazing at the sky above, with his stomach pressed hard against the wall of the Krishna temple in Marathadi Lane, painted in columns of red and white and daubed with saffron. To look at him, you surely don't have to be a writer shouldering the burden of observing the world and recording it, nor do you have to be a humanitarian, anxious about the welfare of your fellow beings. Actually, the Nadar shop owner who buys the scrap from him every day, and cheats him, yet provides him a livelihood—he knows him quite well. Then, too, the aged and bearded chairman of the Krishna Temple Maintenance Association, who sneaks up behind him while he's in his trance-like state with his stomach pressed hard against the temple wall, intensely gazing at the sky above, and whacks his behind with a stick, then cackles his cruel laugh as he enjoys the sight of the man skittering off in shock and pain—he, too, knows him quite well. The old beggar, too, who wraps dirty clothes around his leg to beg and shares his night's sleep in the 'Too Good' bus shed with him (for which he loots part of the day's scrap-metal earnings so that he can buy himself some beedis and ganja)—he knows him quite well, too.

* This is a Sinhalese phrase, which means, 'Our Country'. It is often used as a slogan by all sections of the Sinhalese political parties.

If you consider yourself too civilized to meet him in person, you could always opt to go to the street leading from Marathadi Lane to the railway station, stand in the shade of the magnificent *sirissa** tree, and just watch him. First you'd see a yellow bus, owned by the New Eastern Bus Company, heading off to Irakkakandi and raising a hell of a lot of dust and smoke on its way. Next you let the gas van pass by with its horn sounding like an infant's cry. Then (if you are a male), you shake off your sexual emotions or erotic fantasizing over the girl clad in the light-blue *churidhar* riding her ladies' bicycle behind the van, and let her pass, or (if you are female) you stop pondering the quality of the kitchen larder offered for sale by the loud cries of head-loaders, or momentarily unload your own sincere concern in ferreting out the faults in the moral behaviour of other women, and you look towards the entrance to the Krishna temple. You spot the veiled woman selling peanuts at the gate. Behind her, then, you can see him, standing right up against the wall with his stomach pressed hard against it, intensely gazing at the sky above.

With his dirt-coloured trousers on, his navel protruding from his dark and naked tummy crushed up against the temple wall, he'll be standing there gazing at the sky above. Maybe he was trying to digest the old, rotten food that the shopkeeper palmed off on him, or even better, attempting to pleasure himself by standing there with this tummy crushed against the wall, his bloodshot eyes glowing in that ugly face, gazing hard at the sky. Maybe he stood there gazing at the sky just to keep from panicking at the sight of other people's faces, or maybe it was a well-meant accommodation on his part to keep other people from screaming and running away at the sight of his vicious face. This trance will continue until the

---

* In Tamil, this tree is called '*vaagai*' and its botanical name is *Sirissa olbasia*, known for its wide and beautiful canopy.

chairman of the Krishna Temple Maintenance Association comes and rudely interrupts it.

You would do well to avoid looking directly at his face. Not that his reddish eyes staring blankly out of his dark face would scare you. Rather, it's that on the entire half of one cheek, lined up in a perfect semicircle, at regular, close intervals, eleven pairs of tiny holes would be starkly visible, clutching at his flesh. Those gnawing spots clutching at his tissues are a mix of red and pale yellow, with blood and pus oozing out, feeding a continuous stream of buzzing flies and mosquitoes. He will not look like he's taking in the aesthetic glory of a star-laden night sky—after all, it is still daytime—nor will his eyes suggest anything like that, with their demonic, spiteful look, staring hard at the sky. Shining red just like his eyes, he just stands there, watching a twisting and turning tiny little river in the sky, soaked in red, yet not sticky. It seems like any other river, with no trace of anything gooey or viscous, yet it is stained with a stream of red. To him, it smelt of blood. Worse than the red of the river, he could see a more garish mix of red and white in the bits and pieces of human flesh in it, interspersed with a steady stream of yellow brain tissues, soaking and bubbling in the red river. Rabid black dogs waited along the banks of the stream with their red, glowing eyes glaring into the river, their mouths wide open. Sometimes the dogs jumped into the river, biting and snatching at pieces of flesh and brains, with shreds of tissue dribbling from their jowls. This is how he sees the river running across the sky above.

One day, at dusk, when the scarlet-flushed sky reddened the palm leaves and the neem treetops, a missile fired from the 'Welcome Vihara' Camp fell into the 'Mill' refugee camp where they were staying, and exploded. When they discharged him from the hospital more than twenty days later, they had stitched eleven pairs of tiny holes in a perfect semicircle on the entire half of a cheek. He eventually made his way back to the 'Mill' camp, where he saw only red blood, dried and darkened on the wall and on the cement floor. Chunks of rotten flesh stuck to the walls, still oozing fluids and giving off a foul stench. Maggots wriggled beneath those globs of flesh. After that day he gave up his search for his parents and relatives. During the nights that followed, he tried out the 'Too Good' bus shed to sleep in. He found that it was already claimed by an old beggar who tied dirty clothes around his legs when he begged, as his place to earn his living and to sleep in. Some days, when the old beggar couldn't get his beedis or ganja, he wouldn't let him sleep there. The old beggar had to be sufficiently 'high' to let him share the sleeping space. Still, first thing in the morning when he sobered up, he would kick him out. This meant that he spent most of his nights in the small lane behind the bus shed, between it and the compound wall of the railway engineer's bungalow. He got used to the stench of urine (thanks to people waiting at the bus shed during the day) and to the heat, to the ruffling of polythene bags, and to the grinding of bits of broken glass, and he learnt to ignore the early-morning breeze with its determined chill, so he could get some sleep. But for the last few nights, even when the old beggar was not at the bus shed he stopped sleeping there or even behind the shed. He had taken to a narrow, unused, concrete culvert, under the sirissa trees, as his new night-time abode. A few days earlier, when he was trying to dodge a brick thrown at him by the respected chairman of the Krishna Temple Maintenance Association, which had nonetheless hit his elbow and brought the blood spurting out, and as he continued to flee from the barrage of bricks, he noticed the old beggar in a heated argument with a bunch of 'elder brothers', all sporting the same coloured T-shirts and new caps.

He could see that those 'elder brothers' were carrying political posters, coloured the same as their T-shirts, with the picture of an elderly man, and that they were trying to put them up at the bus shed, but that the old beggar was trying to stop them. The old beggar was throwing a huge tantrum, pacing up and down and shouting. He then saw that all over the bus shed there were other, similar political posters printed in the same colour as the T-shirts. But these pictured a different leader, with two pictures on each poster—one showing him wearing a white dhoti and shirt, and greeting people, and the other one displaying him all dressed up in a suit, and waving his hand.

'Hey, listen up! We got no quarrel with them. We use the same colour and the same symbol as the ones on their posters. It's only the number of pictures that's different. We'll paste ours up below theirs—we won't cover them up. Now, move over!'

'No way! Once honest, always honest! I gave my word to that Sir that I will not allow other posters here. You cannot put them up here. Go on . . . git!'

'You crooked old beggar dog, you . . .'

One of the 'brothers' took hold of the old beggar's neck and shoved him, but the rest of them stepped in and calmed him down. On the ground in front of the bus shed there developed a collage of random footmarks, shoe prints, and dust scuffed around on the dry surface, revealing wet sand raked up underneath. Then they left and walked towards a van parked in the road. That's when he noticed that van. It sported the same colour as their T-shirts. All around the van, there was that same leader, willingly smiling and greeting, with both hands raised above his head. He could see the men's vicious faces climbing into the van and sitting down behind black glass windowpanes when the van started with a jerk. The wheels spun against the ground spewing dust and smoke before the vehicle began to move, and then it suddenly leaped ahead and raced off. For a moment it looked almost certain that it was going to roll over when it bent around the corner by the church, then it disappeared after the turn. That evening he watched as the leader's face on the posters at the bus shed paled and faded into darkness. That night, he smelled an extra stink of beedi and ganja smoke, much more than usual. He also noticed that the old beggar had some new currency notes of different sizes and colours. The leader, whose face had been pervading the entire bus shed, and his colour, had disappeared completely into the dark night. He could not figure out the exact nature of the old beggar's new business enterprise, but he clearly realized that today he had laboured harder than usual.

Well, the old man was certainly smart.

'De, you loafer! Some of your scrap ain't iron, boy . . . just because you can lay your hands on it for free, dummy! You got to tell the steel from the iron. Steel means higher prices, boy! You got to tell the good from the bad, you loafer!'

Later that night, he dreamed of dogs swimming in the faded red river, chewing and snatching at completely whitened bones, floating, untainted by the colour of the river. When the dogs tried to snatch them, the bones slipped out like rubber, regaining their original shape. At just such a moment, he heard the quiet rumble of a vehicle approaching the bus shed and parking. The sounds of footsteps and a certain restrained commotion reached his ears. His thoroughly exhausted body, the stench from the urine, and concern about the bone-snatching dogs would not permit him to get up and look. He stayed where he was. Pretty soon the commotion increased. The clank of iron rods hitting the cement floor and walls of the bus shed could be heard distinctly, right inside his skull. The old beggar's ganja-infested grumbling turned into a growl, peaked, and turned threatening. Suddenly he yelped, howled, begged, wailed, whimpered, and receded into silence. The sound of the van peaked, and then it faded away. As the dogs resumed their smacking, he drifted off, back into sleep.

When the cold dew of the early-morning chill smeared all over his body like holy ash, with weariness, he woke up, shaking off the dogs and the bone pieces. He began to smell something different from the usual stink of ganja and beedi. What's more, it reminded him of the same stench when his 'Mill' camp was shelled. Frightened by bloody rivers and blood-stinking dogs, he peered out at the bus shed. The old beggar was lying there, like a ripped-apart bundle of clothes. He really woke up when he realized he couldn't see the old beggar's head. The old beggar's sarong lay off a ways, not tied around his waist. There were bloodstains and torn skin above the thread he wore around his hips. The old man lay there upside down, with his legs crossed and his head banged up against the wall. He noticed a long, thick, blood-smeared iron rod lying in front of the bus shed. He cleaned the blood stains from the iron rod by rubbing it in the sand. Then slowly, as the old shopkeeper had said, he used the cap of a soda bottle to scratch at it. It was steel. He was happy. He started walking towards the scrap metal shop, proudly carrying the find of his early morning's magnificent labour.

He chose the narrow, empty culvert to sleep in for the next few days, as the bus shed was barren and stinking of blood. It will only be a matter of time before the chairman of the Krishna Temple Maintenance Association will come and chase him away, but until that happens he will stand right there, his stomach pressed hard against the wall of the Krishna temple, painted in columns of red and white and daubed with saffron, and stare hard at the river of blood running in the sky, trying to digest rotten food, or to pleasure himself.

Translated by D. Senthil Babu

V. Gowribalan, *'Appe Ratta'* (2003), in *Oppanai Nizhal* (first edition 2003), Parisal, Chennai, 2010, pp. 89–96

Iron Birds

V. Gowribalan

'Even if you turn a deaf ear to the prophecy of that fifteenth-century prophet—that something terrible would come from the sky, two iron birds would crash into two big buildings, the world would go to ruin, and people would die of starvation—you must surely have realized that, with its production of impotent seeds, this world has dared to deprive itself of chlorophyll. This incident, occurring not long before he picked up those pieces of lead, is recorded here.'

Cheeks puffed out past their ears, hairless, stomachs bloated, legless too, ghosts sunk in the sea come up and beat their heads on the ground, along with the tall waves. Oh, oh, oh . . . bellowed the seashore in the thoughts of a little boy who lived there. With the rumbling of monsoon rains, ocean waves entered the seaside home of a friend of the little boy. The friend's little sister, in a darkened room, clutching a window bar with one hand, her sleepy face covered by the dark so that only her white teeth gleam, is making a racket. Things generally unwanted by the friend's family and himself are banging against the coconut tree trunk in the courtyard, floating on the rumbling salty white foam of ocean waves. A little while ago the friend's father, with a smile, went down the rain-muddied street on his bicycle. So, this is a region where conditions are such that it's possible for this story to happen, a region by the sea that's been overlooked by moviemakers in favour of the city; or maybe conditions are such that it's possible for this story to happen in any region, where any of the world's languages is spoken.

Those objects drew his attention with a kind of perpetually tension-producing panic. Like ink spilled in a new notebook, giving birth to anxiety, like a map of the world soaking into the pages of a notebook, a panic spread right through him, unnerving him. But he felt incapable of diverting his attention, his concentration, from those objects. Yes, they did terrify him, but he took it that those objects were also capable of removing the unidentified weight, or pressure, that was bearing down on him. That's why, between nervousness and fear, in anxiety that someone's attention or gaze might fall on him, even though he sensed that the poor-quality cloth might give way and tear, he put those heavy objects into his pants pockets.

The most blows fell on him precisely on the days he went to school with broken pieces of coconut from the Ganesha temple hidden in his loose white shirt, praying that the maths teacher, who always went around with his yellow-white curls hanging down over his forehead, not come to school, and if he came, that he not hit him. He had lost faith in his own prayers, and in God, at a very young age. His eagerness that his maths teacher should know he had those dangerous objects with him was the reason for his keeping them. During the school tea break, he wanted to take advantage of his classmates' presence all around him to take the objects out, very nonchalantly. They would claim to know all about the weapons they were used in. One would say it was L.M.G. rounds. Another would say it was from an S.L.R. After each one had said a name, he wanted, very calmly, to name a gun they hadn't named, in a tone that suggested he had a lot of experience using it, and put the rounds back into the pockets of his pants. By this means, by means of the other students, he wanted to appear enigmatic to the maths teacher. Generally, the maths teacher expressed an unending hostility towards this class. When he punished them severely, he told them he had dreamt at daybreak that the students of that class, dressed like red Indians, were chasing him with sticks and canes in their hands, and his shoulder still ached with the interminable pain of slamming into a door as he got up and fled from them in fright.

So, at the thought that, if he came to know of the rounds in his possession, the teacher would dream that all the black gods under the neem trees and in the temples, red flames glowing in their eyes, were threatening him with their weapons, he smiled to himself uneasily.

On another occasion he learnt that his father, afraid of being arrested if the army did a round-up, had dug a pit in the narrow gap between the thatched palm fence and the cowshed, and buried the wires his older brother, who was always sneaking around, up to no good, had brought home to siphon off electric current. But he also knew that if he told his father upfront that he had buckshot in his possession, he himself, instead of the rounds, could end up buried just behind the cowshed. He would much rather have his father learn about them secretly, through some other person. If that is how it were to happen, he looked forward to confronting his father with pride, knowing that his father, while pretending to ignore him, would secretly keep a close watch on him.

So he collected his thoughts as he walked through the black-and-blue iron deposits in the gutters, made by the running rainwater.

As he approached the sirissa tree, the walkie-talkie on his hip flashed red and crackled. He immediately crouched against the sirissa-tree fence. His right hand was on his hip. It quickly drew his pistol. Lifting the pistol, he placed it close to his neck. Turning the walkie-talkie on with his left hand, he brought it close to his mouth *. . . over . . . over . . . yes . . . over . . . over . . . receive . . . enemy . . . enemy* . . . Tucking the walkie-talkie back in his waist, he brought his left hand as well up to the pistol, and he backed up even closer against the fence. Enemies out there. His back hurt. He felt the rusting barbs of the wire fence and the buds of the sirissa tree burrowing cruelly into his back. The fact that the area around him lacked the flat outer wall of a fort or a wooden blockade, like in Tamil or English films, caused him regret. He felt himself stoop like a question mark. The walkie-talkie flashed red and crackled again . . . *enemy . . . enemy . . .*

change your position . . . over . . . over . . . Yes, he sensed the necessity of changing his position. He heard something fall to the ground with a crack. He felt something warm splattering his feet. He looked and saw cow dung trickling down.

'I've been looking for that buffalo all morning, who knows where all it's wandered off to . . .' *enemy . . . enemy . . . dangerous enemy . . . change your position . . .* his brain commanded him. Besides the trembling of those white flowers among the brown-and-green leaves of the rosebay, he couldn't see anything in front of him, two hops . . . one step . . . another jump . . . that's it . . . crossing that open space and landing behind the potted plants in one go, he could reach his *safety place, one . . . two . . . three . . .* Two steps, one hop, and another jump . . . He hadn't miscalculated. He felt himself land on something hot and bone-hard, yet also with the warm softness of wool. A feeling of helplessness only added to the load on his mind. He looked up at a blue sky with drifting patches of white, and between them two frightening black eyes, pale-red gums, and white-and-yellow sharp fangs. With an ear-splitting scream, he felt himself straining. A continuing feeble groan and a howl made him aware of the severity of his accident. His body writhed once and subsided . . . his lips were quivering. '*Dangerous enemy . . . Keri Palla* . . .* thank god! My balls are still intact . . .'

The restless rumbling of the sea in the monsoon rains . . . the sound of laundry beaten on the rocks . . . squirrel babies chattering *titter-titt* . . . as he heard all of this, the lane seemed silent, without a sound. After the rainfall at noon, finally the yellow sun began to shine . . . but still duskily, and the clouds had not dispersed. He felt damp earth clinging to the soles of his feet. The yellow sunshine, falling right at the centre of the open space bordered by

* *Keri Palla* is an abusive Sinhala term for Tamil.

the palm-leaf fence between a balsam tree and a guava tree, and reaching down to the grassy floor, lay there like a yellow crack . . . the blackish-green grass seemed to be growing *viru-viru*, covering the entire path. He felt the cool breeze spreading very gently over his body. Suddenly a gust of wind came up, then it died down just as suddenly. Sap from the balsam tree was dripping down on his body, on the crown of his head. With the crown of his head numbed by the falling sap, his body trembling, his penis erect, his heart pounding violently, he cried out spontaneously:

Yellow sunshine's beating down
A mango seed's shaking
Machan's getting a hard-on

'If they slap at me, I'll slip away and come to you. If they swipe at me and get me, take off your wedding chain and keep it off . . .' the male mosquito said to his wife . . . He cried out, overcome with the same fright he felt when he thought of the night his grandma died, the one who'd taught him how to kill a mosquito. But he quickly came to his senses. The door to the bathroom in Ragini's house standing open . . . the window of the goldsmith's house locked . . . on the distant, paved road some people walking alone . . . he was grateful that these various things in the narrow lane lying deserted nearby gave him some relief from the fear that had settled on him. Then he walked on, concentrating on the black-and-blue iron deposits in the gutters, made by the running rainwater.

'Hey . . . Sabesan? . . . could you come here for a minute . . .'

Because of the tenderness in the voice or maybe because he recognized its owner, he directed his attention to the scene with only minimal alarm and no deep inner torment. Vasanthi Auntie is washing clothes, squatting by the low wall of the well. He sees

Sivaram and Sriri snickering and talking about Vasanthi Auntie. Vasanthi Auntie is a beauty, for sure.

'*Aiyacci* . . . move the water from the banana tree to the coconut tree, won't you . . .'

Wanting to establish his manhood . . . to show the strength of his arms without actually showing off, he reached out a hand, naturally, with a farmer's keen eye, and changed the direction of the water channelling into the earth. He watched Vasanthi Auntie, unconcernedly washing clothes, parting her lips and singing: 'Who's got a hard-on? . . .'

As if there were a round-up, the cheroot-shop man hid behind his thatched fence, with lime steaming in the background, lifted both hands above his head, waved them about, and shouted. His heart numbed with alarm, he rolled off the top of the henhouse into a mud pit. There was no way he could escape either the mud or the round-up, so he floundered, distressed. His mother called out from inside the clouds or from behind the sooty kitchen chimney like a disembodied voice . . . 'Hey . . . take your book bag like you're going to school . . .' He ran towards the street from a place almost as familiar, but not quite, as the courtyard of his house. However, the street that came to meet him lay before him not like his familiar gravel road but like a path of sand full of palm trees . . . bushes . . . grass . . . There were a lot of people in uniform standing around with guns. He saw himself standing there too, in uniform, with a gun. Even when no one was looking, it made him scared, wandering around these puzzling, unfamiliar paths. Suddenly, a new path appeared before him. He decided to take the rounds out of his book bag and put them down. Suddenly, Mutthappa spoke hoarsely with a stiffened face, in a tense voice that didn't belong to him, as if giving a command . . . 'You shouldn't open your book bag in front of the checkpoint. They say someone pulled out a bag of betel leaves from his hip pocket when he was standing in front of a checkpoint. They thought he might be pulling a gun on them, and they shot him.' He decided to go past the sentry before he put down the rounds . . . Behind him, just like an elephant trumpeting or a plane roaring, there was this very frightening sound of mingled growling and blaring . . . two rounds in succession . . . like in English movies, two sharp edges stretching out in front . . . glitter . . . glittering . . . glimmering . . . A jeep came speeding by . . . he gave it a close look. The maths teacher sat in the front seat, wearing a *veshti* . . . jumping . . . jumping . . . he shouted, 'That's him . . . that's him . . .' His legs grew unsteady, the roads intermittent. The jeep appeared . . . and suddenly disappeared . . . disappeared . . . appeared . . . But he could still hear that scary growling . . . His throat wouldn't stop burning . . . the class monitor and the maths teacher were crouched in the middle of the thorn bushes. Suddenly, in front of him appeared a tower rising so high it seemed to bang against the sky. Its walls swallowed him up and spit him inside. He fell on his side on a grassy floor. He felt water pouring down roughly on his back. With a betel leaf in his mouth, the Principal is watering the garden. He felt a gentle coolness spread over his body and he looked up in alarm. His whole body was wet. The water vessel placed near his head was lying on its side. He lifted himself up and looked at the table. Like a buffalo standing calmly up to his neck in a pond with only his head out of the water, the book bag was lying calmly on the table. He figured that first thing in the morning he should dig a hole behind the kitchen and bury the rounds. All over town the dogs kept barking. At the thought that they might do a round-up in the morning, he felt a cold tremor spread throughout his body.

Translated by Rebecca Whittington

V. Gowribalan, *'Irumbu Paravaigal'* (2003), in *Oppanai Nizhal* (first edition 2003), Parisal, Chennai, 2010, pp. 56–63

Encounter

Ilaiya Abdullah

you knelt down
on a night of seeping rain
and cried, Amma,
at becoming a refugee.
on the morning after
and at sundown still
you were waiting, Amma,
with dampened eyes
your only comfort
was a palm-leaf hut
you were deprived even of that
camp life . . .
you saw even the weaver bird
and the crow live lovingly
by that makeshift camp
you began the second struggle
between your laboured breathing
and the salty sea breeze
straight through the weft of your thoughts
with hurting feet
I am able to keep walking, Amma
for you . . .
you looked at that moon
and smiled
will it still be the same moon

above the smoky clouds
to the north?
life is grown tangled.
in order to live without cursing your fate
you are driven
to love
Amma, for eight years
the life that ran on
drawing and effacing
furrows in the sand
and disappeared
oh Amma, what is it that you need?
lift my chin and tell me
I need that.
we too need
an ancestral land
we need to be blessed with never leaving.

Translated by Rebecca Whittington

Ilaiya Abdullah, '*Ethirkollal*', in *Pinam Seyyum Desam*, Uyirmai, Chennai, 2004

(The backdrop for the poem is the eviction of Tamil Muslims from the Northern Province by the LTTE in 1990.)

Night

S. Vinodhine

the sea draws down the sun
obscuring the earth
the spreading blackness
gathers even in my room
in the chink of sky
that shows through the window
there is no moon
just a star or two glittering.
I long to feel this darkness
with my eyes and fingers

a time of neither
touching nor seeing
a night that answers none of my questions.
the footfalls of death-gods
parading by
fade into nothing
the song of a flute someone somewhere is playing
comes floating
and soaks my soul.

songlike
the night is speaking with me.

Translated by Rebecca Whittington

S. Vinodhine, *'Iravu'* (2004), in *Mugamoodi Seibaval*, Kalachuvadu, Nagerkovil, 2007, p. 28

Midday

S. Vinodhine

the sun-drenched street lay desolate
everywhere, in everything, its intolerable heat
hidden among the noises of machines
the ear-splitting
sound of snatching souls

the first day
and several days before that
they could not catch him
today they put an end to his life
he said that on the very first day
the will to live burned in his heart
and he stopped drinking.
in the floating heat of the deserted street
with bullets
piercing the eyes tearing the face
his desire came to an end
midday.

Translated by Rebecca Whittington

S. Vinodhine, '*Nedum Pagal*' (2006), in *Mugamoodi Seibaval*, Kalachuvadu, Nagerkovil, 2007, p. 39

My Songs

S. Vinodhine

I won't finish my songs
today
not even tomorrow
when will I finish them?
all my unwritten songs
are in the hands of that little girl
she says she won't give them to me just anytime I ask.
she says to take them
when she's not playing with them.
when I try
while she's asleep,
within the space of a word,
she wakes up and starts to struggle
defeated, my soul hides itself
I won't finish my songs
today
not even tomorrow
for unbeknownst to anyone
they are in the safekeeping
of that little girl.

Translated by Rebecca Whittington

S. Vinodhine, '*Enadhu Paadalgalai Naan*' (2006), in *Mugamoodi Seibaval*, Kalachuvadu, Nagerkovil, 2007, p. 76

After Catastrophe

Faheema Jahan

a bird perched
on the stump
of a felled tree.

today it has
no flight
and no song.
before its eyes
a vast expanse
is stretched out, blazing in the sun.

is it cursing those men
or longing for its own nest?

Translated by Rebecca Whittington

Faheema Jahan, '*Azhivin Pinnar*', in *Oru Katal Nirurril*, Panikkudam, Chennai, 2007, p. 12

Merciless Ones

S. Chelian

the sun was floating in the temple tank

they tied up the sun head-down
hit it with sticks
rolled and pushed it
into the tank

in the cloudless expanse of the sky
rain was falling from the leaves
the tank was overflowing with tears
the utterly fearless little ones
had no mercy at all
they had climbed onto the dead sun
and were swimming and playing

the sky had caught fire
and was burning.

Translated by Rebecca Whittington

S. Chelian, '*Karunaiyum Illadavargal*', in *Kadalai Vittuppona Meen Kunjugal*, Kaalam, Toronto, 2007, p. 16

Those Who Killed Them

S. Vinodhine

in the hands of the night
the city lay hidden catlike
they were so fast asleep they didn't sense
the death in gunpowder
and the stench of their own blood
in the wind mingled with the scent of snakes
that night
did a star fall somewhere?
did a sparrow cry out?
did a barn-owl fly over that house?

they had no sense of it
even in dreams
that came in sleep
it must not have happened
the weapons of sorcerers
who blindfolded the night devoured them
tomorrow they will lie drying in the sun
before the next hunt.

Translated by Rebecca Whittington

S. Vinodhine, '*Avargalai Konravargal*' in *Mugamoodi Seibaval*,
Kalachuvadu, Nagerkovil, 2007, p. 30

Take the Child from Me

Faheema Jahan

I have taken the child of sorrow
you thrust on me
with the unbearable weight of betrayal
and lulled it to sleep on my shoulder

so the child will never wake up crying
I have raised around me
a deep silence
without words of consolation

on the stages I am called to
with all due respect
I am made to sit down on my seat
decorously
with the child on my shoulder
I deliver my prepared speeches
in a humble voice
and descend the stairs
a commended daughter of my city.

in the moment when I cross before you
—when the child slips from my shoulder and creeps
onto yours like a vine—
I lull it to sleep again on the other shoulder.

you have every right
to reach out and take from my arms
the crying child that keeps turning
to look at you
never once did your arms stretch out
nor would I want to give it into the arms of anyone else.

Translated by Rebecca Whittington

Faheema Jahan, '*Enathu Kaimarri Yenthi Kol*' (2009), in *Abarathi*, Vadali, Chennai, 2009, pp. 17–18

Barrel-toothed Ghost

T. Malar Chelvan

my son strikes awake
the night sleeping silent
despite all our tested tricks
his voice alone cries out
to the edge of town.
the barrel-toothed ghost
sets the windowpanes of my house
trembling
but my son won't stop crying.
grandma tries to distract him
with grunts and grimaces
but he won't give up.

* * * * *

the night is cruel now
impossible to write in words
the ghost that's climbed onto my shoulder
is ready at any moment
to destroy my head
he's only an infant
what does he understand?

* * * * *

lie still my son!
lie still my son!
there goes a soldier, my son!
lie still my son!

lie still my son!
here comes old barrel-tooth, my son!
lie still my son! lie still!

in the wind* that comes creeping slowly
there goes her voice . . .
he was lying still.

Translated by Rebecca Whittington

T. Malar Chelvan, '*Anji Maraikkal Pallan*' (2009), in *Uyir Nizhal*,
January-July 2009, Paris, p. 58

* *Solaga Kaatru* in Tamil refers to a strong wind that blows from the south during the months of May, June and July in Sri Lanka.

Burning Nest

Karunakaran

the bird that flies up
out of the wound
takes along
its beautiful flower
its great fire
its sea
its space.

it has not even
the shadow of the thought
of returning home
to its nest.

along the way
it gives up even
its wings to the wind.

this journey beyond pain
fills the nest
with emptiness

in the bird's undampened heat
the nest burns, alone.

Translated by Rebecca Whittington

Karunakaran, *'Thagikkum Koodu'* (2009), in *Pali Aadu*, Vadali, Chennai, 2009, p. 30

Black Dog

Karunakaran

a black dog
blacker than its shadow.

its shadow's silence
is stronger, bigger
even than its bark.

the shadow matches
the black dog's
anger, agitation.

does the shadow-dog have
a sense of scent
and memories of old directions?

the black dog is always leaning
on the shadow-dog.

in the shadow-dog's silence
is the black dog's
spirit.

Translated by Rebecca Whittington

Karunakaran, '*Karuppu Nai*' (2009), in *Pali Aadu*, Vadali, Chennai, 2009, p. 85

The Warrior Who Could Not Part from His Shadow

Karunakaran

when he could not part from his shadow
the defeated war hero
felt abandoned
in unguarded territory.

the closed doors
shut him up in fear
and the open doors
seemed terribly dangerous.

knowing the night to be well guarded
he was startled when the very next moment
it turned into
deep trenches of terrors.

when he saw
the keys glow red-hot as they opened the doors
working themselves into the locks
the keyholes
looked at him and smiled.

that mocking smile that said
in any lock
in any key

there is always a way to open
sank into him
like a sense of guilt.

unable to unite
with the shadow from which he could not part

he severed his own head
sweating profusely
in haste
in fear.

Translated by Rebecca Whittington

Karunakaran, '*Nizhalai Vilakka Mudiyaatha Por Veeran*' (2009), in *Pali Aadu*, Vadali, Chennai, 2009, pp. 97–98

Let's Move on Again, to Yet Another Place

Deebachelvan

the land that survived took you
away and stationed you somewhere.
the winds are gathering on the shore
where you left the sack you meant to take with you.

a war-pinched life
without courtyards to play in
without alleyways for wandering cycles
the ground has taken you away.
the gun that was thrust on you
is eating you up.

our older brother's tomb
was our only property
our brother's dream shattered,
his tomb disintegrated.
at this time none of us
have a house to live in.
like our older brother
and his dreams
we are wandering.

what are we to do with our fate
that goes dragging you
out from under the cover
of frightening nights
when we lost everything and,
worn out, went into hiding

how will you make him feel the heat,
the enemy who sends us on the run?
at an age when you knew
and could understand nothing
you were given a war
the gun given into your hand
is ripening your raw heart
the remaining ground gives itself up to the enemy.

why am I approached
by this kind of a poem
and this terrible night?
in the end after all
my words fall flat.
am I now supposed to write an ode
on the children's battleground?

heading into the midst of artillery shells
should you be shivering?
who dragged you away?
they were like an older brother to you.
your older brother loved you
just as much as he loved our country.

the children are hidden by the guns
mother says.

at this time we have no city either
we have no life.
we who have nothing
are ourselves absent.
still we need you
to eat with us the little bit of half-cooked rice
and boiled lentils.
come quickly
let's move on again, to yet another place

(Dedicated to my younger sister, Vengani, who was taken away by the LTTE towards the end of the war, for battle. She, however, survived.)

Translated by Rebecca Whittington

Deebachelvan, '*Nilam Peyarnthalaiya Vandhu Vidu*' (April–May 2009), in *Aatkaltra Nagarathai Thinra Mirugam*, Uyirmai, Chennai, 2009, pp. 91–92

A Boy's Father Dies

Tha. Agilan

A mother was howling and weeping.
'Please save my son. I need him. Please save his life.'
The disciples were all waiting, proud smirks hovering on their faces in anticipation of becoming witnesses to the impending miracle.
Buddha replied, quietly, 'Lady, bring me a fistful of mustard seeds from a house that has never encountered death.'
Buddha's smile remained unchanged.
She ran through the streets. She ran hard, to save her child's life.
But death won in the end.
Death was diffused everywhere, like air.
Not even one fistful of mustard seeds in this earth which hasn't felt the scent of death.

***

Everyone cherishes the wish to conquer death. Death accompanies us through our entire life, like an athlete on a sports track. It follows us right till the end, when it runs ahead of us.

I want to share certain memories left by the footprints of death, which I encountered along my way. I watched my father dying, sitting right next to him. While the smell of death was lingering in his face, the last words he spoke were meant for me.

I was seven years old. I had had no prior information or experience of death before that day. All I knew about death was from watching funeral processions and my fear of the Chinese firecrackers used in those processions. 'Don't show your hands to the dead body. Your hands will rot'—I was scared of my sister's threats, too. To prevent my hands from rotting, I always, carefully, kept them behind my back whenever there was a funeral procession. Once, when I did show my hands, I also managed to create a ruckus, howling and crying, afraid that they might actually rot away.

Now, my father is dead. Everybody worried when they knew that a snake had bitten him. They circled around him. I didn't understand what was happening. I was stuck amidst the people surrounding him. They all wanted to save my father's life. They lifted him and carried him to the road. They laid him down at the Vairavar temple at the street corner, thinking He would save him.

In those days the Indian Army was camped at the corner of our street. Not just in our street, they were camped at several places. Initially, it was funny. It was funny to watch the Indian Army with their beards and turbans, their strange language and their guns, with long knives. That was the first time I had ever seen guns, and only they had them. I never would have believed that they would endanger our lives. Every day they marched up and down in formation, twice in our lane. That was all. My sister used to scare me, saying that they would take me away if I stood outside when they marched past. But I ignored my sister and watched them marching by. Some of them would call out to me, and I would hesitantly smile. I would be lying if I said I was not scared of the Gorkhas. Their beards and turbans would naturally incite fear in anybody. Despite that, I did watch them in fascination.

My sister used to narrate stories about the Gorkhas, tales of their bravery and the chapattis they ate. Those tales just made me fear them more, and hate that mysterious, unknown item of food called chapattis. That's how powerful my sister's tales were. But one day, despite all these things, I was lifted up by an Indian Army man, with a turban, at a totally unexpected moment. Ironically, I suppose, that event helped me to realize that I could actually look quite charming, even though I am dark—charming enough that this Indian Army man wanted to pick me up. But when he did, I started screaming so loud that all the mothers ran out, and he put me down. I blabbered hard, as if I had just escaped from a crocodile's mouth. He tried to pacify me. Afraid that he might lift me up again if I stopped crying, I screamed more. He suddenly took out a yellow balloon from his bag and gave it to me. I quickly grabbed it and gradually lessened the intensity of my howling. But I continued to cry till he left. He walked away, smiling. After that, I did not trust anybody's threats. After all, they give balloons. How could they harm anybody?

But just for a few more days. From marching down the lane, they started to move into the fields. They trampled our crops with their heavy boots. Our uncle, who used to curse us if we walked in the fields with sandals on our feet, stood mutely in silence, watching them. Then they started to cut down the fences along their way. Uncle used to fence his fields to keep the cattle out. They cut them down; but new fences kept springing up, each day at a new place. My uncle finally gave up fencing once and for all, exhausted from the effort of fencing over and over again. That was when I began to see the cruelty in the faces of the Gorkhas, matching with the tales of my sister. I stopped believing they carried balloons any more.

Suddenly, one day they brought their hatchets and destroyed all the fences in all the fields. They cut down entire tree branches, leaving the trees totally bald, every one of them. They installed lights in the bigger trees, painted them white. They said that this is how the trees should always be, and any leaf or branch sprouting out should be cut immediately. In total, they were not like before at all. Actually, it kind of helped me in a way. My mother could not find sticks from a fencerow to punish me with. But my aunt was more worried: there would not be a single stick for her to lean on during the next rains.

One time they stopped a cart carrying thatches for the house and dumped them all out on the street. We were asked to carry them, one by one, from the street to the house. Several restrictions of this kind continued. They started to decide everything—when to light the lamp at home, when to put it out; when people should go out and get back. One day, a jeep roared into the lane and opened fire at random. My mother and I hid under the table, while she prayed to the Ammalachi goddess for our lives, over and over again. Father ventured to look out from the veranda. The next morning I heard father and uncle talking about how eight people were shot dead at the Iranai Madu junction. After that incident, they started laying barbed wire barricades in the streets at six in the evening. Everybody had to be back in their houses before six. No one should be found on the streets after six. That was the first time that I had to light candles for St Anthony on my birthday at four o'clock. I had always done it at six-thirty, for my previous birthdays. That changed too, after the arrival of the Indian Army, and the barbed wire. I asked my mother why they would not allow me to light candles, even on my birthday. As usual, she told me to shut up and pulled me along. Nobody could be out in the streets except military vehicles.

Now, it was well after six-thirty. The Indian Army had already erected those barbed barricades. The only way to take my father to the hospital would be to remove them. Several people were trying to negotiate with the Army, to allow my father to get to the hospital. I could only hear their voices and listen to them begging and crying. The voice that cried the most must have been my elder uncle's. I could only see people's legs. 'Sir, Murthy sir, it's a snake bite, sir,' somebody cried. But the Indian Army refused, vehemently.

I was getting crushed, stuck among people's legs. I managed to reach my father, struggling along the way, tangled up in legs. Father was laid down at the Vairavar temple. I touched his moustache and sought his attention. He hugged me back and cuddled me. It was heavier than usual, his cuddling. Why is my father crying? 'Father is going to God. You must study earnestly,' said my father, his voice trembling. I could not understand the finality and permanence of those words then, but those were my father's last words, and they were spoken to me. I didn't realize, then, that it was that solitary kiss, and those words, that would substitute for every other memory of my father, extending their reach through the rest of my entire life. To tell you the truth, I was totally unaware that death would not return people. The Indian Army refused to permit my father to go to the hospital. Father died. Vairavar gave up too.

Father was brought and laid out at home. I didn't know how many people were there, hugging me and crying. I did feel a bit uncomfortable, but I felt no grief then. I didn't even know grief. I went close to my father and looked at him. For a moment, I felt as if his eyes opened and shut, just once. I definitely saw those pale eyes, and the unbearable pain in them of leaving us behind. I thought about telling someone about my father's eyes, but no one seemed to bother. There were lots of people, too. I wandered around, constantly bumping into people's knees. Finally, I reached my elder uncle and told him about what I saw. He bawled. He hugged me tight and cried out loud, standing in the hallway between the verandah and the kitchen. At that moment, I did feel a little grief in me. I ran, tearing myself away from my uncle. As far as I was concerned, I had seen my father open his eyes. I didn't try to tell anyone else about it after that. Now I regret that. These days I tend to think of it as an illusion. But the little Agilan sitting inside me refuses to consider it an illusion. This big Agilan tries to believe it was just an illusion, but how could the memories of an illusion get stuck in one's heart for twenty years?

People wailing tore my ears off. Then, it all happened quickly. Since father was a dead body then, or this dead body was called my father, I was cautious enough to keep my hands to my back. I wondered though, if my hands really would still rot since this was my own father. I remember well when several people handed me printed homage cards for my father. I sat on top of a sack and read them aloud with the tone of a public announcement. I was trying to imitate the voice of those people who would announce a death to the public, with loudspeakers tied to a car. I was also carrying the betel plate around for whoever asked for it. It still did not register in me then that there is no longer any such a person as father. My elder sister took me away and fed me. I remember the food, bread and curry, and my sister feeding me and my little brother, sitting at our aunt's place. Someone came and asked my sister not to let us go inside, since mother's grief would only deepen if she saw us. My sister nodded in agreement.

I never cried, right? But sitting on someone's shoulders and carrying the funeral pot around my father's body, I suddenly realized that there was something extremely dangerous happening. I began crying. At last, when I saw the dancing, yellowish fire catching on the curly hair on my father's forehead, as he was lying in his silk dhoti and shawl on the pyre, and when I realized that he is never going to come back, I screamed out loud. I recognized at that moment the loss of such a huge support as that of a father. People hugged me, pacified me, gave me soda. Those cries are still lying inside me, dormant. As I write this my lips are trembling, and my heart is engulfed in a subtle tremor.

Now, eighteen years later, when I sat down to write this piece, I thought I was going to record my thoughts about death. But how could I ignore the death of my father? My father was a hazy image to me, not steeped in my memory. But his death did have a deep impact on me. Even more than me, it affected my little brother a great deal. Even worse was the impact it had on my little sister, who was just born then, and who never knew our father's face. While free sympathy for being a fatherless son accompany me all along my way and causes me pain, it fosters his memory in me as well.

Translated by D. Senthil Babu

Tha. Agilan, '*Oru Paiyanin Appa Irandu Ponar*', in *Maranathin Vaasanai*, E. Pathippagam, Chennai, 2009, pp. 21–27

(This essay recollects events that took place during the presence of the Indian Peace Keeping Force in Sri Lanka, from 1987 to 1990.)

A Refugee's Motherland

Ki. Pi. Aravinthan

18-05-2003, Sunday

Early morning telephone calls for people in the Tamil Diaspora in Europe or anywhere else in the world always meant picking up the receiver with a quivering anxiety. Mostly these calls at dawn came from India or Sri Lanka, often carrying unhappy news. It was through one such call waking me that I received word of my mother's death. Was it expected? It is difficult to say. I had just spoken to her for several long hours on Saturday, that is yesterday, a week after she was hospitalized due to a cardiac arrest. She was recovering when I hung up. She had been comforting me, saying that she was to go home the day after next, that she was expecting me and asking me to be sure to come and visit her. Actually, I had already started preparing for the visit from the moment I heard about her emergency admission to the hospital. I had requested the necessary certificate from her hospital's administration stating that my mother was being treated in their Intensive Care Unit. They had informed my mother about that, which made her certain about my visit, making her happy. I wondered if that happiness might have shown her the way to her death. She was overwhelmed by a desire to see me. She was always very affectionate towards me, not just because I was her eldest son, but also because I was the lost sheep in the flock. It had been thirteen years since I separated myself from her. Actually, it's been thirty years since I moved away from the life that she had imagined for me. After 1972, much of my life was spent in prisons and in hiding. She had had to wait for me at the prison gates of Jaffna and Colombo. I knew that this gave her unbearable pain. Even so, it soothes me to think that I had given her happiness on at least three different occasions. First, when I announced my willingness to get married. Worried as she was about my wayward ways, this must have been a great relief to her. Second, when in 1993, my poetry collection, *Mugamkol*, received an award and I arranged for all of the award money to go to her. Her worry that she had never received financial help from her elder son was a bit salvaged by that. And third, when she heard her son's voice on one of her favourite international radio stations. My mother had this habit of listening to the radio, propping it right next to her pillow at night. This was actually one of the reasons that I agreed to participate in a serial programme on BBC-Tamil, when they approached me in 2001, despite my being wary for several other reasons. In truth, this gave her a great deal of happiness and satisfaction. So I did manage to do those things for her, at least. After I started living here, and she in Triconamalai due to my sister's posting there, there were fewer letters and more conversations over the telephone. During such conversations, she repeatedly expressed her wish to spend her last days with me. Even during our last telephone conversation, yesterday, from the hospital, she asked me to stay with her for at least a month, and to take her from Triconamalai to Jaffna.

There is this warning included in the blue document issued to refugees: 'A person who has once taken refuge in another country cannot return until there is lasting peace at home.' But in France, they allow one visit, in dire circumstances. I had planned on using this opportunity to visit my mother, so I had already submitted my application, with all the required documents. They said it would take a week to receive a response to my application, which did not inspire confidence and left me sad and disappointed. Mr and Mrs Durai and Mr A. Murugaiyan had assisted me in submitting those documents. But now this Sunday morning message changed everything. I was shattered and my voice failed me. My brothers tried their best to pacify me over the telephone. But who dealt with their sadness? Sumathi managed to field all the concerned calls from friends. Had I betrayed my mother? Or had she deceived me? All these questions and more churned inside me, and my tears kept gushing out.

19-05-2003, Monday

I could not sleep at all that Sunday night, and I was the first person at the District Administration office on Monday morning. The moment the doors opened at nine, I met the immigration officer to whom I had earlier submitted the documents and, with tears in my eyes, I asked him to let me know his decision as soon as possible. I also submitted another paper informing them of my mother's death on the previous day. My hands were a bit shaky, probably with the sense of urgency that was in my heart. The officer was not harsh in his reply. He told me to go ahead and prepare for the trip, and that my permission would be granted on Wednesday. It now became certain that I could go home.

On 22-05-2003, Thursday, at nine-thirty in the morning, Sri Lankan time, I landed at Colombo airport, accompanied by my brother, who also lived in France. He travelled like me, since both of us were living there as refugees. They had given me my travel permit on Wednesday morning. My refugee card, the token issued to refugees, and other documents were taken by the authorities as guarantee, only after which did they issue my travel permit. According to that permit, my stay in Sri Lanka was limited to just fifteen days. This not only added to my sadness, but I also felt that I was being unfairly treated; my brother had been granted a month. Obviously, the rules vary with departments. I could not sleep through the entire night's flight. Mother's image persisted in my vision. My mother had served as a nurse until she took voluntary retirement. In addition to her burdens at her job, she took on additional service responsibilities, as I had urged her to do. Due to my activities, she also faced problems at work. As I think about all that, guilt washes through my heart. Further preparations to fly to Jaffna from Colombo on the same afternoon had already been finalized. The immigration officials struggled with our French travel permits, in the absence of regular passports. Finally, after inquiries and visits by higher officials, my brother and I were the last to get through the immigration formalities. Then it became certain that I would see my mother's face, in person. My childhood friend Jayamurugan was waiting outside, ready with the travel arrangements. We were to go straight to the domestic airport at Rathinamala. It was still difficult to believe that I was standing in Colombo. We started off to Rathinamala from Kattunayaka through Colombo city. As we were entering Colombo, I realized I was feeling giddy. The city started looking muddled, and in retreat. I began to wonder if I was going to die even before I got to see my mother. I told my brother to let my friend take care of me, and that he should proceed to Jaffna as planned. I was gradually losing control of myself. I slid over onto my brother, sitting next to me, while the driver drove the car around in search of a hospital.

23-05-2003, Friday

When the domestic flight touched down, running on the Palali runway, I shivered inside. My friend was next to me, but I did not let him know about my shivers. I closed my eyes. I am going to see my mother, in my hometown, in my motherland. In the midst of this swelling turmoil inside me, the doors of my subconscious burst open. My brain seemed to melt and ooze out. Aren't all these things real, right in front of me, sprawled out and soaked in the hot sun, as sand and stone, as plants and trees, as bushes and palms, keeping me yearning and active? I look around in awe, gazing at my mother, who nourished my life with her breast milk. I touch the earth and smear it on my eyelids.

The van started towards Jaffna town, rattling and leaving trails of dusty red sand behind. Looking out, I tried to identify places, but in vain. These were the places, the little villages, the tiny lanes on the route of bus number 764 from Jaffna town, where I used to wander. But I could not identify a thing till I reached my village. I could not even identify the north Punnalai Kattuvan junction leading to Kuppilan village, a place that I enjoyed and had grown up with ever since my school days. It was simply ruins and destruction, all around. The van hurried us towards Urumbirai junction. My eyes were searching for the statue of Sivakumaran. Wasn't he like the source of a turbulent river? Wasn't he the one who planted fire in the tree-hole in the midst of the forest?* But my eyes couldn't locate his statue. Memories of the times I spent with him between 1972 and 5 June 1974 rose up within me: Sivakumaran's mother had been the first to come forward, smothering my head with her hands, asking about my health. She fed rice to me and to Sivakumaran. How many mothers had fed us like that, with compassion? They were the first to realize their children's sense of justice. I saluted in the direction of their house. Eventually, the van stopped at the bus terminus near the farm. I got off. It was a place that had sprouted anew. Bushes sprawled in place of the Jaffna Fort. Hailing a taxi, I gave the driver my address. The taxi rolled along, past Veerasingam Hall behind the Jaffna Library. There stood the fort built by the Dutch, holding the Jaffna prison in its belly. The Jaffna police station that once stood at its entrance like a secure, fortified gate had disappeared, all traces of it perished into an empty, barren, deserted field. The breeze from the Pannaikkadal

* Echoing the famous poem of the Tamil poet Subramania Bharathi (1882–1921).

blew in through that space. The wretched final-day events of the Fourth International Tamil Studies Conference had been staged right here, in front of Veerasingam Hall. Pillars once erected in remembrance of those wretched memories lay there now, spread all over, in ruins. I was witness to those wretched final-day events, which unfolded on 10 January 1974. I was serving as a volunteer. Sivakumaran was in charge of our volunteer group. Sivakumaran and I were standing next to the dais. Our group had prevailed upon the conference coordinator to stage the meeting out in the open. Enraged by what had happened that day, Sivakumaran and I pledged to take revenge that same night, while we were clearing up the premises. My mother waited up for me at home, which I reached well after midnight. Several people from my street had gathered together. A teacher who lived close to our street had lost his life in the incident. It still feels like it's just happening all over again today, when I remember the relief shining on my mother's face when she saw me, and the compassionate inquiries from my neighbours. In that incident I somehow lost a wrist watch that my mother had bought for me, but the ring she had given me was safe. Mother was not worried about the lost watch. But she was glad about the ring. She had given me that blue-stone ring when I was released from prison in 1972, to banish my bad characteristics and to bring me well-being. One of her colleagues who believed in such things must have given her this idea. I am not sure if the ring helped in allaying my bad characteristics, but it was definitely useful for me later. Once, when we didn't have enough money to buy a revolver, my mother's ring and my friend Padmanaba's ring, both had to be sold. When I returned home that dusky evening, my mother was startled not to see the ring. I managed to cook up some excuse to tell her. Now, I can't stop my tears, sources of the well don't seem to dry up at all! Memories engulf me of the first day my mother came to visit me in this fort's prison, with my two-year-old youngest sister, after I was arrested on 18 May 1972. My mother's pain, due to disappointment and shame, showed clearly on her face. I was a political prisoner then. I used to wonder why my mother was broken, instead of being proud. But when I went home after I was released six months later, I was struck by the practical reality of the social attitudes towards prisons and the police. I could relate to the ways in which my mother had been hurt. But there was no change at all in the way she showered love and compassion on me. The fact that she called me Manoharan, the eldest of the seven children she gave birth to, must certainly be because of a dream that she cherished within her. None of my relatives knew that my real name was Francis. They still call me Manoharan. My mother must have been influenced by the movie *Manohara,* released in 1953. But did I live up to her expectations of a dream son? Or did I become a son who betrayed his mother and the motherland? Time will tell. When I was arrested for the second time in 1975, I was made out to be a dangerous terrorist. On the second day of my arrest, I was subjected to the inquiries of the Jaffna Crime Intelligence department. Two weeks later, I was sent to Velikkada for the Colombo interrogation. I was severely assaulted, stripped naked, and made to sit on a chair. I responded to the questions they shot at me. Inspector Padmanadan and his deputies—Shanmuganadan, Karunanidhi and Rodriguez, among others—stood surrounding me, angry and furious. A typist was recording my testimony. I could see my mother, worn out, running along the side of the street towards the office portion of the police station. Yes, I was looking at her. I was also aware that pretty soon, they would bring my mother in here. I knew the pain she would go through if she saw me in this state. I wished they would hide me. But it was their intention to make my mother see me that way. The entrance wasn't that far. Mother reached the entrance. I turned my face away. She was not permitted to talk to me. What must have been her state of mind? Later that evening, they locked me in police custody and gave me a parcel that my mother had brought. Food that mother had packed for me was wrapped in a newspaper published on the day of my arrest. I took a moment to acknowledge my mother's thoughtfulness. There have been so many other times when she acted thoughtfully like this, on her own. Memories of my mother keep gathering in me. How is it possible to pour them all out? The taxi was hurrying past Subramanya Park and the court complex, towards home. It was in this court complex that Sub-Inspector Chadrasekara pinpointed me in an identification parade. Near the end of 1977, arrest warrants were issued on me for several cases, including this one, but I kept coming home. I attended the trial of the first case, and bail was granted until the next hearing, but only on surety of land or cash. We had neither. I was sent back to jail. It took ten days for my mother to mobilize and pay the money. She sold all the jewels in the house, including her wedding chain. On the way back home, she said, 'Son, there are still two more warrants. We have no way to handle them. You better discuss it with your comrades, or go underground and continue your activities, as before.' After that I never attended any trial for any case. Those words still guide me today, I guess. I still avoid being in the light. I keep assuming new names. I still like being underground, being the dark horse.

When I finally arrived and could really look at her, I was completely taken over by the emotions of seeing my mother. I stood next to her head. All our relatives were sitting around her. Candles were burning. The room was filled with wailings. My brothers and my father stood next to me, holding each other. I could not cry. 'Cry out loud, my son,' said my father. The bright face of my mother was covered with a thin towel. Pushing it aside, I caressed her. What should I cry about and to whom? Or would she like me crying at all?

24-05-2003, Saturday

Today is my mother's birthday, the beginning of her 75th year. She would leave the house that afternoon. Kith and kin had gathered to bid her farewell. We did not consciously plan to cremate my mother on her birthday. When she died in the Triconamalai hospital on 18 May, my father had her brought to our Jaffna home that same day. My father was determined to keep my mother's body at home until all her children arrived. My brother living in Norway had left on Tuesday and the other brother living in Germany had left on Wednesday. Though my other brother and I had planned to reach Jaffna on Thursday, and he arrived as planned, I couldn't make it until Friday. This led to the decision to cremate her on Saturday. My mother had asked my father and her youngest daughter-in-law, Devadana, to take her to Jaffna in case something happened to her. My wife, Sumathi's brother Dananjayan was astonished when he went to organize clothes for my mother after she died. Her suitcase was packed, all ready to go to Jaffna. She had made her preparations to leave for Jaffna even before she fell ill. She had even written to the tenants at our Jaffna house three months earlier, requesting them to be prepared to hand over the house to her in May. She had closed her bank account in Triconamalai and handed over the money to Kesavan, another of Sumathi's brothers. Such precautionary measures!

The time arrived. The final rites began. My father was the first to garland mother, followed by sons and relatives. Neighbours, people of the village my mother loved, walked around, paying their last respects. Whimpers could be heard. I started the farewell speech. 'Dear All! My mother has lived, thanks to all your love. You all are well aware of how our mother brought us up. We and our mother shared mutual affection. But the fact that none of us, her seven children, could be with her during her last days, will continue to haunt us all. My mother stayed committed to love, compassion and service to the cause of others. This is what she taught us. We will continue to live, trying to deserve all your love. Except for her certain grief that her children were not next to her, our mother died happily. All has gone well.

'Let us bid farewell to mother. Good bye, mother!'

Each of us caressed her for the last time. The cart bearing mother began to move. My mother continues to be around us. After the funeral, I was in the midst of relatives, neighbours and friends. Only then did I realize how precious the moment was. It was an opportunity to witness a cross section of my society. I took this as my mother's gift, even in her death. I began the second leg of my journey, in search of my motherland.

Translated by D. Senthil Babu

Ki. Pi. Aravinthan, '*Oru Agathiyin Thaayum Thayagamum*' (2004), in *Iruppum Veruppum*, Salaram, Chennai, 2009, pp. 100–109

Immense Land: An Introduction to Its Soil Strata

Pa. Ahilan

beneath the big city
buried in weeds and myths
water and homes
the dayless, nightless, tireless streets
and the branches spreading thickly

the surface abuzz with hurrying people
and speeding vehicles
if you descend

striking steps
even beneath this
if you keep descending
leaving
the surface of a storm of ashes still warm
even beneath
the close-laying sound-strata of crying and screaming
even beneath
the liquid bed of unstaunched blood
even beneath
the stratum of thought already thickened, dense, full of thorns

if you keep descending
even further down, leaving
the great expanse of silence untouched even by the roots of trees

an ancient woman
an ascetic on a throne of skin, scattering the times.

Translated by Rebecca Whittington

Written in 2010

Pa. Ahilan, *'Peru Nilam—Mannadukkugal Parriya Arimugam'* (2010), in *Saramakavigal*, Peru, Jaffna, 2011, p. 45

Story of an Unwritten Letter . . .

Na. Sathyabalan

the flame is flickering in the lamp
not knowing
it is struggling, doubting
every moment it faces
distress flickering in the prayers of the one who lit the lamp
who tells the flame to endure the pain of living
the wick resumes its austerities, composedly absorbing
the oil, which is running out
the heart of the lampstand that bears all this
is throbbing

a gentle light diffuses and fills the room,
overflowing, thronging prayers struggle for breath
striking and bouncing off the walls, doors and windows.
not knowing how to write to the wind
to submit their prayers
the flame and the wick suffocate
the moments roll along and dissolve

Translated by Rebecca Whittington

Na. Sathyabalan, '*Ezhudhappadaadha Madalonrin Kathai*' (2010), in http://marupaathy.blogspot.in/2010/09/blog-post_2958.html

Little Brother

S. Chelian

Right in front of Miss Prahaspati and all the thirty-seven kids in my class, Principal Rajagopal brandished his cane whip and whacked me six times on my butt. What was so special about the number six? Not my classmate Ramachandran, glaring evilly at me, not Miss Pirahaspati in her wrath, not the rest of the class, subdued as they were, not even me myself, standing there stiff, with my brain curdled, none of us ever really figured that one out. Maybe it was just Principal Rajagopal's lucky number. But in the history of our school, the Navalapitti Kathiresan Kumara Maha Vittiyalayam, nobody else, even today, can possibly have matched that record—six whacks on the butt.

Of course it's true that teachers cane students on their butts in order to 'correct' them. We hear all kinds of stories about students squirming and quivering, or collapsing in a heap. It is even believable that scars from some of those canings are still there today, on some people's butts. There are stories making the rounds to the effect that some of these brave souls have secretly received the noble title of 'Great Man of Valour' when they related these brave sagas to their wives. Perhaps our United Nations General Assembly could be petitioned to look into these violations of human rights, since they occurred in Third World schools. The unemployed need something to do, don't they? However, we surely can believe that our government is not prepared to permit the United Nations to do any research into the condition of its people's bottoms. Besides, those brothers might well think they'd rather die than look at such stuff. Still, we shouldn't just blurt out whatever comes into our mouths about how the United Nations is a hapless, tainted organization. At least until it comes to the point where it decides by majority vote whether or not it is okay to rape women or to rape men, we can believe with some certainty, or at least have a bit of faith, in it as a 'democratic organization' and a Protector God for the Earth and for all the people who live upon it.

That day I was accused of the crime of writing disrespectfully about Members of Parliament—Arulambalam, Rajan Selvanayagam, Thyagaraja, Minister Kumara Suriyar, and Mayor Thuraippa—in my handwritten magazine. My handwritten magazine was confiscated and I was sent for an interrogation in the Principal's office by my classroom teacher Miss Pirahaspati, through the dutiful services of a student, by the name of Ramachandran.

The Principal called me in for the interrogation during our lunch break. With the Vice Principal right there, he thumbed through the magazine, and said, 'He has written all this stuff about these respected ministers.' He seemed astonished. I have no idea what he really thought, but after a couple of minutes, he let me go. One possibility was that the image of my father's face might have come to him at just the right moment.

This, however, was intolerable, not only to Ramachandran but also to our classroom teacher Miss Pirahaspati. They marched right back to the Principal. What they talked about remains a great mystery, but as soon as lunch break ended, here came the Principal with his long cane. He imagined his cane was born right along with him, like Karnan's famous armour. Our class teacher Miss Pirahaspati came along too.

'Who wrote these essays? Who did the drawings? Who authored the poems? Whose handwriting is in this magazine?' The Principal asked lots of kinds of questions, but I had no difficulty in replying, since they all had the same answer.

'I did all of it, under different names,' said I, and the people who actually did draw the drawings, write the poems, and write the short stories all heaved a sigh of relief. When the interrogation was over, the Principal decided on caning as my punishment. In truth, though, that punishment had been decided upon even before the inquiry.

Before executing his decision, Principal Rajagopal asked me to face the wall. Was that so the other students could more easily see my butt? Was it because he didn't have the guts to watch my face while he was caning me? I do not know. Not a single teardrop, through all six whacks. But after that, my heart just refused to identify with that college* any longer. I had already been planning to go to Jaffna for my studies, so the next year I enrolled at Hindu College, again in the eighth grade.

One morning as I was going to college there were bands of a few young men blocking the paths of the students and turning them back. 'Today is a day of mourning. Boycott school,' they said. They didn't bother with me, though. This was a complete novelty to me. I had never seen anything like it. The college was deserted. A few students were huddled together, talking.

'What's going on?' I asked quietly.

Clearly agitated, they replied, 'Diraviyam is dead.'

Everybody's face overflowed with grief, as though they had just lost a close relative.

'They say Diraviyam robbed the Copay Bank and as he was making his getaway, the police caught him. So he took cyanide and died,' explained one of them.

'So, who is this Diraviyam?'—though my heart was aching to ask, I was reluctant.

'Diraviyam needed the money to buy a gun,' said another.

'All the guys who were with him got away—he's the only one who got caught,' somebody else said.

* High school.

'It was those people in Neerveli who caught him and turned him over to the police. They just didn't know who he was,' said somebody in anger.

Who is this guy? Why are these students so upset, and the teachers confined to their rooms? And the young men standing in the streets?

'Diraviyam was none other than Sivakumaran,' Ranjith whispered discretely into my ear. 'He rose up as a militant—he believed that only armed revolution would bring freedom from ethnic oppression. He bombed a police officer. He has been living underground somewhere around here, and the police have been going crazy trying to find him.'

Sivakumaran's body was brought to Urumbara for cremation. Usually whenever somebody died in the town the funeral procession would pass by my house. A hundred or two hundred people might walk past. But for Sivakumaran's cremation more than two thousand people marched through the street in front of our house. And not just people from my village, either. Young men and women from villages all around Jaffna rallied together. The cremation ground lay just past the end of our land, where palm, guava and thorn trees mushroomed in utter freedom, completely at their will. I climbed to the top of a tall guava tree and watched the last rites of this hero born in the trenches of our motherland. This Sivakumaran showed us new pathways when he was alive. But even after he died he scripted new ways to live. According to Tamil tradition, women are not supposed to come to a cremation ground. They just come up to the fence. But here at Sivakumaran's funeral, hundreds of women gathered inside the cremation ground and wailed out their grief. Not only that, but a joint cry went up from all the people who wanted to see Sivakumaran's face one last time. Traditionally once closed, the coffin was not allowed to be reopened for anyone to look again at the body. But here, bowing to the wishes of the people, his body was raised high into the sky by several notables, including P.U. Navaratthinam, and shown so that everyone could see. When they saw his innocent, childlike face, everyone fell into an agonized rapture. Tears flowed from every eye. From a few people's eyes not one tear dropped, though: they stared deep into him, and determination grew in their hearts.

Finally, about ten feet from the foot of the guava tree I was sitting in, that hero's sacrificial body was fed to the fiery flames. I watched the glowing fire for a long time, from my perch in the guava tree. I did not feel like going back home. Eventually, though, I found my way to the house of a relative who shared our well.

'With my own hands, I gave water from our well to some young people coming back from paying their respects at the deceased person's house,' said my cousin Lali's husband. 'They swore to take revenge.'

I was glad to hear that.

Contrary to tradition, a memorial was built in that Hindu cremation ground. Pon Sivakumaran was the name that was etched on it. Every year, Sivakumaran's mother lit lamps and showered flowers upon it. Sometimes our household donated water and a grass-cutting spade.

One of those days over a thousand young people rallied and walked past our house, heading for the cremation ground. I was standing in our doorway, and I joined them and went to the cremation ground. They paid homage to Pon Sivakumaran at his memorial. I learnt that these young people were from the Tamil Youth Assembly, and that their leader was Santhathiyaar. I also learnt, from Santhathiyaar's speech, that after paying homage to Sivakumaran, they were going to head out, on foot, to attend a final campaign rally for the Kankesanturai by-elections at Mutruveli, shouting Father Selva's slogan: 'Tamil Ealam is now our collective destiny!'

I followed them in a trance. Following Santhathiyaar's orders, we marched two-by-two along the sides of the streets. When I walked past my house, no one came out to stop me. Led by Santhathiyaar and walking along the sides of the streets we posed no problems for the traffic, and people emerged from all of the homes we passed. When they saw us they gave us their heartfelt best wishes. From some of the homes people served us water to quench our thirst. As we passed Kondavil corner in Palaali Street, suddenly there were police jeeps blocking our way. I was standing just two feet behind Santhathiyaar, and I got a bit scared.

The District Assistant Chief of Police in Jaffna climbed out of one of the jeeps and questioned Santhathiyaar. He could not speak Tamil, and Santhathiyaar could not speak Sinhalese, so the police officer spoke in English. Santhathiyaar said that he did not know English. Another police officer was given the task of interpretation.

'It is against the law to take out a procession without a permit. Disperse immediately,' said the Assistant Chief of Police.

'This is not a procession. We are walking to the election rally because we have no money for bus fare.'

'This is against the law. You are creating a traffic problem for ordinary people.'

'We are not causing anybody any trouble in the streets. We're walking along the sides of the roads.' That was Santhathiyaar's reply.

After a few more minutes of talking, with Santhathiyaar not backing down on anything, the police jeeps turned around and drove off. Our crowd roared in joy, and we continued our march. When we came to the Tirunelveli Agricultural Association building, a car blocked our way. Out came a visibly angered Thalapathy Amirthalingam Anna.

'What is the meaning of this, Santhathiyaar? What did you promise the police officials, in my presence? How could you break your promise and lead this procession?'

'Anna, this is not a procession. We did not have enough money for the bus fare, so we are walking,' said Santhathiyaar, unperturbed.

'Okay, if that's the way it is, I'll send you all to the rally right now,' said Amirthalingam.

He raised his hand and brought to a halt all the cars, buses, and other vehicles driving down Palaali Street. At his request, they dropped whatever had brought them to Palaali Street in the first place, and all the cars, buses and other vehicles took us in and delivered us to the rally. In ten minutes, we were all there.

'Little brother, get in my car,' said Amirthalingam, patting me on the shoulder, and one of the other passengers helped me in.

We all participated in Father Selva's final campaign rally. The thundering voice of the rights of Tamil people rose to the heavens that day. Some fifty thousand people took part in that rally. It was ten o'clock at night when it finally wound down. To this day, I cannot recall how I made my way home.

'What have you been up to till this odd hour of the night?' was not a question that anybody in my family asked me. Only our dog jumped up as soon as he saw me and wagged his tail, in silence. Even he knew how to behave, late that night.

Translated by D. Senthil Babu

S. Chelian, '*Chinnathambi*' (2010), in *Kaalam* Journal,
January–March, 2010

Restless Sea . . . Sleepless Land . . . Endless Dream

Karunakaran

A life surrounded

within me a restless sea
before me a sleepless land
and so this unsubsiding anger
everywhere an unending dream . . .
in my eyes a fire rises
a river flooding
people turned into stone slabs on the roadside
for others to rest their loads . . .

in the street filled with people ripped and flung
today a god is born
the stroke of midnight is muffled by
the unsubsiding fire . . .
the stray cows and the compounds
overgrown with jungle
and the streets thick with darkness
in the taken towns there are more soldiers than people
if you want to go home, ask a soldier for the address
get permission from him
and find out from him about me

he must be finding out about me every day, the soldier
never about my tears

about the burning kindled within me
about my growing into a jungle
about the aching wounds on my body
about my suffering days without sleep
he'll never know.
about the type and the location of my excrement
about my having yawned, he has found out.

what's more
the confusion and fear taking hold of my legs
and the surveillance over my eyes and head
even if you can spot it in the soldier's eye
you too will be silently placed inside
a circle of surveillance and sent to me

even in a time without war
my life and days are hemmed in by investigations
a restless sea within me
a sleepless land an unsubsiding anger
everywhere an unending dream . . .

in my eyes a fire rises
a flood rises and runs out as blood
the people turned into stone slabs . . .
in the distance the sound of a bell
announcing the birth of a child
echoes on the holy crosses

Translated by Rebecca Whittington

Karunakaran, '*Oyaa Kadal . . . Urangaa Nilam . . . Theeraa Kanavu*' (2011), in Karunakaran, *Oru Payaniyin Porkala Kurippugal*, Karrupu Pirathigal, Chennai, 2012, pp. 90–91

Yugapuranam: Myth of an Era

Nilanthan

Part I

it was the end of an era
the rain fell out of season

people fucked with abandon
the earth's youth exhausted,
the wives of the sages
had gone to the forest for penance*
false prophets had cropped up everywhere
and were roaming around in every street
selling tall tales.

it was a lie,
all that talk of a little boat
coming to carry seven sages
across the ocean of milk.
it was a waste,
all that time spent waiting
for wonders and marvels
a nation
promiscuous in war

* 'Before the beginning of the Bharata War, Vyasa went to his mother and said, "Mother, the earth's youth has been exhausted. Now go to the forest to perform penance."'

called on its firstborn children
death was waiting like a creditor
on the steps of a bunker
the arms of strong men
had withered with guilt
the false prophets and the charlatans
had already surrendered
and the grateful people, oh,
they'd become cannon fodder
only those who think with their blood*
stood alone, unscarred

a beautiful heroic era
with its puzzling heroism
and its unparalleled sacrifice

vanished, sunk in the mud of the seashore.

Part II

a nation that did not value upright men
dogged the heels
of blind believers
only those who think with their blood
amassed imperial pleasures
not a single soothsayer
lived there.

* Otto Van Bismarck, who unified Germany, used to say 'Germans should think with their blood.'

in a nation that asked for nothing else
but victories in battle
there was a famine
even of coffins
there was no one
even to dig graves
death seemed
even more certain than life
whenever the cannons
were seized with hunger
the people
were not hungry
were not thirsty
had no pleasure
did no penance

there was no one to eat

the discarded fruits

those were cruel days
weapons were blunted
or bounced back
all those who thought with their blood
went off to the heaven of heroes
and oh, the people who gave up their firstborn children
became prisoners or refugees
on a day given up
even by loving people
the unparalleled hero
his unparalleled sacrifice
expired

a rare heroic era
with dreams frozen in its eyes
and garlands of fading sirissa
vanished, sunk in the mud of the seashore.

Part III

In Nandikadal lagoon
man from Vanni once more became a refugee
from among long-gone corpses
from among
rejected prayers
he came fleeing.

the ashes and tears
of those who disappeared,

the hopelessness and curses
of the people whose trust was broken
the last dreams
of those who were betrayed

clung in his eyes.

between the big sea and the little lagoon
the nation shrank to three tiny villages,
between victory and a hero's heaven
the future pushed on, uncomprehending

people fleeing with nowhere to go

stumbled

on their own corpses and prayers.

the murdered are the lucky ones
the traitor's badge is not for them

for the imprisoned
and the wounded who surrendered
ayyo

for the man who swallowed defeat
and lost his limbs
ayyo

for the man who cooked seeds and young rice plants
and the man who lit the cooking fire
ayyo

the garland of withered sirissa
hung in the bald palmyra trees
could not break free
the big sea
wailed
beating its chest

the arecanut bird
sang with blood throbbing in its voice

caught on touch-me-not thorns
the dream of the man from Vanni quivered
on the dull walls

of roofless houses
the heroic era is beaten flat
but the shores of the Nandi lagoon
do not give in to the stench of blood
and the reign of wildflowers
sends out new shoots.

Part IV

enemies capturing herds of cows
women crying out for protection
Dvaraka sinking into the water

Krishna is missing

since that was the end of an era

the warlords were strongest

the warlords cropped up everywhere
and lightened the load of the earth

withering, drying up with grief for their sons
on the banks of the Yamuna
Yadavas clash with Yadavas
Sinhalas clash with Tamils
Sinhalas clash with Sinhalas
Tamils clash with Tamils
Muslims clash with Tamils
Sinhalas clash with Muslims
on Kudumbi mountain

in Kaththan Kuti
in the Verugal river
in Nandi lagoon
the pennant of victory wet with the blood
of its own brother
throbs without shame

the sound of the warlords' snores

is heard ripping through the nights.
a little boat
bearing seven sages
pushed off into the sea of milk.
hiding on the riverbank, Krishna
weary of playing
his epochal game,
must be in a yogic sleep
to ease his fatigue

the river of time

gulps down and digests

the subject-matter of a heroic era

the potter of time

dissolving the ashes

of a heroic era

on that very water bank

threw earth on his wheel and began

a new era.

the eternal music of the changing eras
comes oozing out
of the corpse-laden
banks of the Yamuna.

Part V

am I
a solitary heron suffering
in the dried-out pond by the seashore
for times that do not come?

am I not even more ancient
than the roots of the banyan tree
where the cobra lives
on the seashore?
I am
the granary of abandoned villages
I am
the biggest merchant
of this roofless capital
I came to sing an elegy
for an era old and dead
I came to recite the epic
of an era newly born
I am the jester,
the Shakti of the era

descended into my hymns
the Maya of the era
returns my years to me

where is my sacrificial hall?
where is my sacrificial horse?

now
the days to come are mine.
Krishna!
give me your flute!

Translated by Rebecca Whittington

Nilanthan, '*Yugappuranam*' (2011), in *Ini Enathu Naatkale Varum*,
Vitiyal, Coimbatore, 2012, pp. 93–99

Keep All That to Yourself

Karunakaran

there came a saying:
if you have faith
then all will be well.

there came an order
that said: fear nothing.

there came a call:
be patient,

there came a warning:
keep peace,

there came an appeal
to relinquish everything.

I was everything and with everything
even when nothing came of anything

even when I found out
where all these came from
whom they came for
what they came for
keep all this to yourself
and leave me

to go my way gently
as a snail
as an ant
and why not even as a human being.

Translated by Rebecca Whittington

Karunakaran, *'Neeye Vaiththiru Avarraiyellam'*, in *Oru Payaniyin Por Kala Kurippugal*, Karuppu Pirathigal, Chennai, 2012, p. 30

The Sea and Dreams

Ki. Pi. Aravinthan

the sea is deep and beautiful
and primeval
and unlike ponds and lakes
and like a dream, limitless.
the sea spread with waves
and the dream yearning for freedom
there was a time when
they were fused together

in starless darkness
on the fathomless dream's sea-surface
many rowed in search of direction.

boats of those bearing dreams
fell into the hands of those
who refused to support
the rowers with tired arms

roaring raging tireless
waves
yet unwilling to move away from
the sea.

would you believe
that these very waves
issued by this very sea
have eaten my dream?

I have a story of escape
from the waves of the sea
with the dream's remainder brimming over
despite this struggle
and the scars of narrow escape
I love the sea deeply
even today.

all that rises must come down
this is no new law
and neither is drifting along
the wind's direction a surrender.

tales in all directions
of the rolling sea
with its tireless waves
of insatiable fury

little waves within me too
rise up foaming and overflow
suddenly one day
the dream of the sea
breaks and scatters

in the fixed staring eyes
lying curled in the Mullivaykkal*
it has gone stiff
in the waveless depthless
stagnant sea
of the Nandi lagoon†.

Translated by Rebecca Whittington

Ki. Pi. Aravinthan, *'Kadalum Kanavum'* (2012), *Kakkai Cirakinile* Journal, May 2012, Chennai, p. 3

* The place of the final battle between the LTTE and the Sri Lankan Army in May 2009.

† Nandi Kadal, the lagoon in which the LTTE leader V. Prabhakaran's body was found in May 2009.

Madakkombarai in Jaffna: A Memoir*

Malliappu Santhi[†] *Thilakar*

I reserved two bus tickets for my friend, Lenin Mathivanan, and myself on the 16th, well ahead of our trip to Jaffna on 19 July 2013. Despite being a seasoned traveller, having been to many countries, this trip was constantly making me restless and anxious, like never before. The main purpose of my trip to Jaffna was to speak at a literary conference on 20th and 21st July. I have been a teacher early in my career. I am currently a management consultant. Public speaking or a presenting a paper usually does not make me anxious. The reasons for my anxiety about this particular trip, however, were different.

I was born on 29 September 1973 in the Lion Quarters of the 'Puthukkatu' division of a plantation called Madakkombarai near Vattakkotai town of Nuvarelia (Nuwara Eliya) district, as the fourth child of my parents. (The eldest child, Chandrasekaran, died before he was a year old; the other two were my elder sisters.) It was on the day the government provided half a measure of rice to each family as relief against a famine that haunted Sri Lanka.

---

* (An extract from a memoir about an upcountry plantation worker family that shows the interconnections of this migrant Tamil community [of more recent origins than the Jaffna–Vanni–Batticaloa Tamils] of workers with the rest of the regions.)

† Malliappu Santhi (literally, Jasmine Junction) is an important landmark on the Colombo–Kandy highway, before Hatton. Strategically located, it is the only way to enter and exit the upcountry plantations where Tamil workers live. Historically, the junction has been the site of several important labour struggles and agitations.

A year or two before I was born, my father's father, *thatha*, had moved, with his family, to the Killinocchi–Vattakkatchi region of Vanni. Time led part of his family of plantation workers to Vanni and made them farm labourers. My three aunts and an uncle (my father's younger brother) were among those family members who moved. Our own family, along with another aunt and two uncles, continued living in Madakkombarai, in the hills ('upcountry'). Later on my eldest uncle also moved, with his family, to Vanni. The rest of us visited them from time to time. My memory of the very first time I made such a trip with my uncle, in 1978, when I was five years old, is still fresh. It was the first time I had ever seen my grandfather and grandmother (*appayi*, as grandmothers are called in the hills, became *aacchi* when I met her, probably because of the Vanni connection).

In 1979, because of my acquaintance with the Sinhalese families in the PWD quarters located by the side of the pathway leading into our plantation, I wrote the Sinhala alphabet before I even learnt to write my first Tamil alphabet (*ayanna* before *aanaa*), sitting on the mud floor of our Madakkombarai (Vatakkimalai) plantation school. Even before that, when I could barely remember my own age, I had become familiar with the Tamil primer of letters, the *Ariccuvati*, in the 'night school' of the neighbouring house where Mr Megharaja, an uncle of mine, now based in Kunnur in Salem district, Tamil Nadu, used to live. Since then, I have always called my uncle Megharaja my guru.

In 1977, although the government changed, our starving didn't. A biscuit in the morning and steamed *chou-chou* (a popular vegetable in the hills) for lunch and, if the budget permitted, a little rice for dinner; this was how our days passed. As poverty chased us, the only way for my father to fend it off was to move to Vanni himself.

Witnessing the ethnic violence of the times, internalizing someone's 'far-sighted vision' that 'if one had to live in this country, the Sinhalese medium of instruction was the only way', our father enrolled three of us in the Vattakkadai Sinhala school. This meant bidding farewell to the dhoti-clad Gopinath Master from Jaffna (he had a penchant for pinching hard the back of our thighs if we were found guilty; from hearsay I gather he lives in France these days), Master Arumainayakam (from Batticaloa, I think), the school supervisor (*kankaani*; plantation schools also had a supervisor!), old man 'Vatthangi', several friends, and even the slates and chalks that marked the beginning of our tryst with letters. To teach us Sinhalese letters, we had Sinhala teachers like Menikke Teacher, Amarakkon Teacher, Sarat Sir and Vidana Sir, among others. From Matiaparanam and Gunaraja, friends from the mud-floor Madakkombarai plantation school, now in Vattakkadai, my friends were Ravindre, Nandasene, Indike, Iyasene. Everything had changed.

Occasionally, a money order from father would ease our hunger. His letters inspired us, gave us solace. He would write interestingly about happenings in the country, with a certain 'pride'. But poverty dogged our family. Mother's daily wage helped a bit. Not just my father, my mother, too, received her share of 'far-sighted vision' whereupon we were sent packing to evening tuitions to learn Tamil after school. 'If we learn Sinhala, won't tomorrow's children need to know Tamil?' So, when the Sinhalese school day was over, he enrolled us in night tutorial sessions to learn Tamil. Thus, as soon as it got dark, we presented ourselves at the Vattakkadai Sri Krishna Social Welfare School. Mister Shanmugam, the teacher and director of that school, became another guiding force in my life. He writes in the *Suryakanthi* magazine under the name of Vattakkodai-Subbaiah Rajasekaran. He helped relieve my hunger, gave me an education and enriched my life.

There is no need to write about July 1983. While Tamilians were burning, I was studying in the third grade, in a Sinhalese school. My friend Ravindra, during some spat or the other, called me a *Para Thamila*. The very next instant my hand flew up. Ravindra, bawling with a bloodied mouth and a broken tooth in his hand, and I stood before the Principal for interrogation. I was giving my statement in Sinhala. (Just as we all do now . . .) Vidana Sir spewed hate as he looked me over. Sarat Sir looked at me with compassion. And the bell rang for school to close. 'Tomorrow the inquiry will continue,' they said, and sent us away. As the three of us were filing out, Sarat Sir took us aside and spoke affectionately. 'You'd better not come back to this school ever again. I am telling you this for your own good,' he said. We took our leave of him in the customary Sinhalese way. He blessed us and saw us off. Even today, the image of him dressed in white shirts and trousers, his curly hair and sharp nose, and his smile, remains with me. Sarat Sir was large in appearance and also at heart.

When father's far-sightedness was reduced to bits in an instant, mother's far-sighted plan came in handy. Shanmugam Master took us to the Vattakodai Tamil school, introduced us to the headmaster Shanmuganathan, and explained what happened. The headmaster thought for a while, then sent for the third-grade Tamil textbooks, and asked us to read. Standing straight, legs taut, I read aloud, breathlessly. Patting me on my back with a smile, Shangmuganathan said, 'Here (in this Tamil school), I doubt if a fifth-grader would read like this,' and looked at Shanmugam Master, who explained how, at my mother's request, I attended 'night classes' at his private school. I looked at Shanmugam Master in gratitude. 'Didn't your father come with you?' asked the headmaster. 'Father's working at a rice mill in Jaffna. We are at home with our mother. Our uncle has come with us,' I said, pointing at my father's younger brother, Tharmakularaja. The headmaster asked, 'Which town in Jaffna?' Uncle replied, 'Kokkuvil.' So father after all went to Jaffna, not Vanni. I remembered getting excited about seeing the name 'Kokkuvil' on the envelope containing his letters.

'Oh . . . I'm from Inuvil myself. I don't see why you should run around here when you could pursue your education there. Till then, I will admit you here. Write to your father about this,' said the headmaster. Enrolling us in the Vattakodai Tamil school, he too had imposed his own 'far-sighted vision' on us.

I must have studied at the Vattakodai Tamil school for about a month. Then, just like our kin in the plantations, who would knock at every door to inform everyone about their returning to India (*homeland*) under the auspices of the Srimavo–Shastri Agreement, we did the same and moved to Vanni. Along with my sisters, I was put in Killinocchi's St Theresa's School (at that time boys could also study there till the fifth grade—I don't know how it is now). I don't know if this involved yet another far-sighted plan of father's, or there was some Machiavellian game behind my not being admitted into the Kokkuvil Hindu School, though father lived very close to it. The talk by Professor A.C. George in a panel on casteism at the 41st Literary Meet, 2012, for which I went to Jaffna prompted me to check with my father as to why I was not enrolled in Kokkuvil Hindu school.

The days in Killinocchi and Karadippokku, at St Theresa's School, affected me a lot. When we lived in the hills, I had to live apart from my father, but now I was without my mother as well. We were made to stay with an aunt in Vattakkachi, to go to school, while my parents stayed in Jaffna, where they worked. We did frequently visit Jaffna. I remember the Tamil film songs of those years played on the bus trips to Jaffna, the voice of K.S. Raja hosting film-based programmes on the radio, in particular. I also remember the Tamil movies that our uncle would take us to in the different cinema halls (Shanthi, Windsor, Manohara, Raja, Rani).

We were given a tiny house at the edge of the huge concrete floor-slab, built to dry rice, at the mill. The floor was big enough for us to ride on cycles as we wished. The compound wall hid the narrow lane that led to our house. There was a tamarind tree behind the house. If we climbed up on the roof, we could eat as many of its fruits as we fancied. On the left-hand side of the house there was a drumstick tree. Mother's preparations from its drumsticks remain unforgettable memories of that Jaffna home. Going back to school in Killinocchi after holidays wasn't easy. Tears would well up as I trod reluctantly towards the classroom. It wasn't so difficult at the Sinhalese school at the plantations. I was a product of that Sinhalese elementary school and I did not know any of the Tamil 'technical terms' of the classroom. Still I would speak, read and write 'Tamil'. For example, when those students said '*alirappar*' what came out of my mouth was '*ma(k)kanee*'. Both meant eraser. But the trouble is that the former was Tamil and the latter Sinhala.

I am a Tamilian. But I felt everyone looked at me as though I were Sinhalese. I would sit on the last possible bench in the classroom, almost always close to tears. I had, however, one dear friend. I still wish I could meet him somehow in this lifetime, my friend Nesakumar. He was from the Kandy Teldeniya region and had suffered due to violence there. Since he had come from a Tamil elementary school, he knew all these Tamil 'technical terms'. I was a lot more at ease when I was with him. Somehow the final year examinations came and I managed to score well, passing in first class. Not sure how I managed a seat at the front row in the next class. However, I was a lot more fluent with the Jaffna Tamil terms, so much so that I could easily say not just '*alirubber*', but also '*pendu*' (then), '*cycle ulakki*' (to ride a cycle) and '*velikkittu*' (to go out). Even in those days, I remember going to a popular Rajinikanth film at the Eswara theatre along with my cousin, Senthooran.

As time was racing along like this, one day, because of heavy rain the Iranaimadu reservoir got breached and the water surged to destroy all the small bridges between Vattakkachi and Killinocchi. We went to school in the morning, but we could not return home later. The villagers struggled hard and, with a Herculean effort, built some catamarans that took us home, scared to death all along the way. Going to school was often interrupted. Father's illness made it impossible for him to return to the North from Madakkombarai, where he went visiting. Mother had to get to Killinocchi, making our stay with our aunt even more burdensome. Unhindered by anyone's 'far-sighted vision', this time around, we returned to the hills, for good.

Again, Shanmugam Master, the headmaster Shanmuganathan, and the Vattakodai Tamil school. I had left there as a third grader, and now returned in time for the fifth grade exams there. I could not do well in that exam and had become considerably 'weak' (as a student). By now my speech had a whiff of Jaffna in it. Bhagyalakshmi, Gomathi, Mutthulakshmi, Gnanambikai, Bhavani, and . . . some other female teachers whose name ends in '–mani', and Indrarajan the maths teacher, whom we all called by the nickname 'Kotthurotti', they were all teachers from Jaffna working in that Vattakodai school. Bhagyalakshmi Teacher staged a play in Jaffna dialect in that Vattakodai school. I played the part of a government agent *(vithaanaiyar)* and received compliments for good acting.

Within a few days, my hill-country Tamil came back to stick to me, but not the school itself. Then Uncle Dharmakularaja enrolled me in the Puntuloya Tamil High School, where he had studied. I joined the school just when the headmaster Nataraja left, after being promoted. Later, after I had grown close to him, he'd laugh and say that I gave him his promotion. There, too, Gukeesvararaja (commerce), Irudayanathan (Tamil), Rajaratnam (mathematics), Muralidaran (science) and Vignesvaran (class teacher) were teachers from Jaffna. Teacher G. Muralidaran was a good artist. He adapted Professor Mounaguru's play *Rain* as *Eyes Seeking the Dawn* and directed it, featuring me. That play won national recognition in the Tamil Day celebrations. It was on the way to stage it at the national competition that we were compelled to turn back, because there was a bomb attack on the security minister, Ranjan Vijayaratne, near Nittamby on the Colombo–Kandy highway. Later, during my school days it was staged at the National Literary Festival, headed by P.P. Devaraj, when I was selected as the best actor.

The year 1989 was marked by the Janatha Vimukthi Perumana (JVP)-led riots. It was a time when tea factories were burnt as they were seen as symbols of foreign investment, disrupting the foundations of the Sri Lankan economy. I also remember the JVP's arguments from those times, that the tea-plantation workers were leftovers of Indian expansionism. In the forests of Madakumbaram on the way to school from Madakkombarai to Punduloyaa, several times I have seen burnt corpses of people, with charred tyres around their necks. In fact, I was the one who ran to inform the village about the killing of the Madakkombarai camp manager Dharmaraja, a Tamilian, who was shot dead by the JVP, a bullet in his head. I found him on the roadside, on my way to school. His gravestone can still be found at the same spot where he was shot, near the entrance to the village, as a symbol. Just a kilometre away from there, on the roadside, is the tomb of the people's poet and leader C.V. Velu Pillai. The JVP problem was at its peak in the South and the Indian Army had just left the North under the regime of President Ranasinghe Premadasa. The Tigers were often visiting Colombo for talks. Vanni seemed secure, once again.

In 1990, I took the public examination and returned to Vanni to pursue higher studies. This time, it was just me. It was a time of many changes, thanks to the departure of the Indian Army and the Thirteenth Amendment*. I reached Visvamadu, where another uncle and aunt were living. I was thinking of going to high school in Murasumottai or Kandavalai, and stay with an

* The Thirteenth Amendment (13A) to the Constitution of Sri Lanka created Provincial Councils in the country. This also made Sinhala and Tamil the official languages of the country, and English the link language.

aunt. We had land at Visvamadu as well. While helping my uncle out in his farm, I have seen fighters of the movement walking around with guns.

One day as I was riding my bicycle to our farm along a narrow lane, I was trapped at the junction of three streets by three cyclists bearing guns, and I couldn't move in any direction. I was scared. 'What's your name? Where are you coming from? Why are you coming along here? Do you have any connection with E.P.?' Many questions were asked. I stood there in the midday sun. I had seen them going around in the streets before, so I figured they must be Tigers. A few minutes after I thought they had finished their interrogation, making way for me, they said, 'Okay. You can go.' I bore down on my bicycle pedals, trembling with fear and reached the farm, and I narrated the entire incident to my uncle. Listening to me quietly, he said, 'Is that so? . . . Let's go somewhere immediately.' He went out somewhere with a sense of determination. The radio was announcing the death of A. Aziz, the president of the plantation workers' union.

My uncle came back and I was ready. Both of us left on his bicycle, with him riding fast. I could see the schools in Murasumottai and Kandavalai passing me by on my bicycle ride. I had no clue where I was going. There I was imagining that my uncle was taking me to certain big shots of the movement to set my record straight, and was even enthusiastically pushing pedals to assist him. But he was in no mood to talk. It seemed as if he was thinking of reaching some place much before anyone else did. He spoke only after we reached the Parandan railway station.

'If they know for certain that you have no connection with anybody, you'll have no trouble. But that by itself will fuel trouble for your family. You're the only male child of the house. I know of only one way out. I have to send you home,' he said. That was when I realized that the reason he was in such a hurry was to catch the 'Yazh (Jaffna) Devi' train. I arrived at Vattakkodai by way of Polakavalai after I had been able to get a glimpse of St Theresa's School, where I had previously studied, from the train. How two police posts came up around our Madakkombarai house a month after I arrived is another story. But the Yazh Devi train which set me down in Polakavalai that day never went back to Jaffna again—to this day. It has resumed its operations after the war but has only managed to touch Vavuniya and Tandikulam. It is now contemplating about going to Killinocchi. The fact that I was on this bus going to Jaffna even before the Yazh Devi was causing me so much anxiety and restlessness.

What foresight on the part of my uncle too! Having left Jaffna on his advice, it has taken me twenty-three years to cross Vanni and now twenty-seven years to return to Jaffna. In between, my cousin-brother Devaraja has committed suicide in Vanni. Another cousin, Tiruchenturan, who took me to the movies, has been buried as 'Nithi'.* Cousin Shanthini has been sowed as 'Poonkuyil'. Who would know that all of them were born in Madakkombarai and were carried to Vanni as infants? My railway man uncle Thangaiah fled with his sewing machine when people were asked to leave during the final phase of the war. When he could no longer run carrying the machine, he had to abandon it midway, which made him feel utterly ill. We rescued him from 'Arunachalam' prisoner's camp and tried to treat him, but he did not recover and died subsequently. We buried him in Madakkombarai . . . once again.

How could I be at peace with myself on this journey thinking about all these?

I continued my journey chatting with my friend Lenin. He fell asleep, but I couldn't sleep. Anxiety kept me awake. Determined

* Both 'Nithi' and 'Poonkuyil' are their noms de guerre, referring to the fact that they died as martyrs in the war.

not to get off at Vanni and to proceed straight to Jaffna, I continued on the bus, tracking the scars on the landscape, despite the driver's best attempts to frighten me to death. Though annoyed with his driving, I decided to remain calm, as I was going back as a new person. There were other journalists like Devagowri, Dushyanthini and Kesha on the same bus. But nothing much transpired by way of conversation between us. I hardly knew them then.

As soon as I got off the bus at Jaffna, I went to the place where the literary conference was going on and did not move an inch till it got over the next day. In the first session on the second day, I spoke on Poetic Literature and Nationalism of the 'Upcountry'. In the final session the same evening, my friend Lenin Mathivanan spoke on 'Upcountry Nationalism'. Our plans to leave the same night seemed to fall through. We postponed our trip by a day and shifted elsewhere for the night. Friends Acura and Devadoss embraced us warmly. We visited Raghavan and Nirmala on the way there. Devadoss sat on top of a table and started singing the hill songs popularized by EPRLF*, while Nirmala and Sumathi started singing the songs of Meenatchi Ammal Natesayyar†. A proper concert had begun. Cheered on by Kovai Nandan, Asura, Raghavan and Lenin, I started singing the songs of Vattakkodai Kabalichellan, the lesser-known, legendary 'Upcountry' folk singer. (It wasn't even a month since he had died.)

Songs with a beat made friends like Nirmala dance. She was pleasant and wished me well, like my mother would. It was a surprising coincidence that away from the literary conference, a musical evening was in progress, comprising only 'Upcountry' songs.

---

* EPRLF, Ealam People's Revolutionary Liberation Front, was one of the militant organizations with left leanings supported by the Government of India, and suppressed by the LTTE.

† She was a well-known trade union activist of the hill-country workers, and a writer. She was married to S.K. Natesa Ayyar, (1887–1947), a pioneering trade unionist among the hill-country workers, and a journalist.

It was the morning of the third day. After twenty-three years, I bathed with water drawn from the well. The morning felt nice. Breakfast with friends. Lenin and I set out to go around Jaffna as I had told him I wanted to. 'No problem. We'll go wherever you want to go,' he agreed. We boarded the bus to Gangesanturai, and I told the conductor, 'Drop us off at Taavadi.' From memories I had carried inside me for the last twenty-seven years and inquiries at the roadside garage about 'that rice mill', we approached that lane in the hot sun. The lane ends at the mill's gate. As I reached the place, I was restless. Lenin seemed to understand my emotions.

The concrete floor where I used to cycle was overrun by bushes. I was searching for my house. I could spot the remains of its foundation. Holding back tears, I went to the miller who informed me: 'They sold it to us a long time ago.' The area where our home used to be had also been sold in bits and pieces. I asked about the water tank that I was so fond of. The stranger said, 'There it is,' pointing in a certain direction. I asked if I could take a picture. He said he would check with the owner. We decided to avoid the trouble and I just took a photograph of myself along with the remnants of what was our home. So many old memories flooded my mind at that moment that I could think of nothing else.

It must have been 1984. As a ten-year-old boy, I loved my holidays, when I could hang around my mother; carrying buckets of water from the garden, and the joy of collecting warm rice as it fell from the mill, not to mention the food made of that warm rice in those days. I used to love running to the shop often.

One day as I went to the shop, a few older boys on cycles in a group, gave me some handbills. I had no idea what were in my hand, as I was waiting my turn to buy some chilli powder from the grinding mill at the corner. Then a loud thundering noise broke out . . . thud . . thud . . . People started to run, screaming. I looked out into the street. The old man of the shop, Veerappa, asked me to run home to tell my family that the army was coming, hunting for those brothers distributing the handbills. As I was running in the lane, I could see a cow rolling over, dying from a gunshot wound? Bolting the compound gate, I ran to my mother and told her about what was coming. We gathered whatever we could and stepped out of the house. My father was working in the mill, a bit inside. The owner's mother came out of her house, which was next to the mill. She saw us panicking. As we were telling her what had happened, a family was banging on the gate that I had bolted tight.

'The army is coming . . . shooting . . . Please save us . . . Open the gate . . .' cried the family in terror. There were about six of them, including wife, husband and children. I could recognize them as people living in one of the mud huts by one side of the narrow lane leading to the rice mill, so I ran to open the gate. 'Don't open that gate, boy! Do not open that gate!' the owner's mother stopped me. The family was trembling. Crying. Begging. But the owner's mother kept on scolding me. With fear lingering in me, after seeing the cow get shot and roll over and die, her harsh words only scared me more. My mother pulled me close to her and hugged me. I was totally focused on opening the gate. The sound of gunshots started getting closer. . . .

One of the men in the fleeing family, shirtless, his lungi tied up to his thighs, had a small knife tucked in at his waist. That tall, dark robust man climbed up on the gate and jumped inside, pulled at the gate and, with just one yank, the lock broke. The gate opened. They entered the rice mill where we all stood, now in greater number. In their hands were ladles, knives and cooking utensils, and in the little ones' hands were bicycle tires they'd been playing with. They must have just fled instantly. Now the sound of the approaching army was fading. The narrow lane had two to three turns. The army did not venture beyond the second. They must have seen the desolate houses and left. But the fleeing families had spread over the entire mill. The owner's mother was cursing herself, beating her head.

It was common among the plantation workers to use abusive language, and the children were not immune to it. But my own mother had kept me away from all that. But the tall, dark man who climbed over the gate came close to the owner's mother and said, 'Talking about caste, what caste? #@*&*# caste . . .' and he hurled the choicest curses at her. My mother could not keep me away from those abuses. In fact, I realize now that I was rather enjoying them. Everyone who had left the mill, including my father, the workers and us were watching, as if it were a drama. I could not understand much about the events of the day then, until I could hear the speeches of writers like Theniyan, Senior Gunasingam, Akalya, Devadas, Rengan Devarajan, A.C. George, and the anxious and tense reactions of the conference organizer Vel Tanjan. Sarat Sir from the Sinhalese school even now was hovering in my eyes.

Rescuing myself from memories, Lenin Mathivanan and I walked towards the KKS Street. Visited the Jaffna library and the Nallur temple. But couldn't even go inside them. The library was closed on the full moon day. The temple was closed after the day's ritual. We went to the new home of our friends. The house where the musical evening had taken place the previous night apparently was maintained by them as a memorial for their sister Rajini Tiranagama*. After spending some time there, we returned to the old house. Having come prepared to stay for just two days, we had run out of clothes. Our friend Asura pulled brand-new shirts out of

---

* A professional doctor and a human rights activist, she was assassinated by the LTTE. She also co-authored the book *The Broken Palmyra* (The Sri Lankan Studies Institute, Claremont CA, 1990), chronicling the abuses of both the IPKF and the LTTE in Jaffna. There is a documentary film on her—*No More Tears, Sister*, directed by Helen Klodansky, 2005.

his luggage from France. I felt a new bonding with Jaffna. Full of emotions, we bade goodbye. Asura and Devadoss, who had come to see us off at the bus station, took leave of us. We got into the bus after a mini-shopping trip to get *odiyal*, dry fish, snacks from Paruthithurai, *idiappam* trays, pickled chillies, palm jaggery, and other assorted snacks.

On the way back, it felt as if my friend Asura was jumping out of my shirt pocket, teasing me. As I reached home the next morning at six, the first question that my mother asked was: 'How is our home in Jaffna . . .?'

Translated by D. Senthil Babu

Malliappu Santhi Thilagar, *Yaazhppanathil 'Madakkombarai'* (2013), in *Jeevanathi*, No. 63, December 2013, pp. 39–47, published from Nelliady, Jaffna.

Release

V. Gowribalan

Stepping back a bit as she walked behind the bus moving ahead, its dense, dark smoke choking her, she stood there, clearing the smoke with her right hand. As she got off the bus, she had worried that her light, nylon churidhar clinging to her body with sweat, was disgustingly revealing it. She grew angry as if the stench of arrack from the stout lips and thick moustache of the man who fell on her, had settled on her body too. She felt her attention shattering, unable to focus her thoughts on the landmarks that layered her memories, as the intermittent heat and the sweltering wind slapped her face. She felt the throbbing pain rise on the left side of her forehead as her headache flared up, reminding her of its latent presence. She felt sad that the crumpled bag tucked tightly under her left arm, made out of a fertilizer sack, had left herself and her community wandering in an ancient time. Wrapping one end of her white *dupatta* around her left arm to hide it, she put the other end around her neck like a garland. She sensed her feeling an implacable anxiety as this was not her familiar narrow road, with its potholes and its sweeping white sand. She was distressed as she felt alienated, insecure and alone standing on that wide tarred road, with its clear white stripes rising from the white sandy surface. She realized that she had got off the bus, two stops earlier, because of the rush and the panic induced by the fact of her coming here after a long time.

She bowed her head down into the burning sun right on her eyebrows decayed and dissolved as colour bubbles in her watering eyes. She felt, just like her, the tall electric post's shadow lying humped and curled up inside the pit. She stood there feeling uncomfortable in that churidhar, clinging to her body with sweat, bought for someone else. She felt disgusted wearing that worn-out purple churidhar, with coloured black dots, that someone else had liked and bought. She remembered she was the last person to pick it up, thinking it would fit her, from the heap of clothes dumped on the cement floor of the rehabilitation camp, from bags made of fertilizer sacks. She saw the goat that came out on the side of the '*eecham*' shrub, going back into it, as it saw her.

Disgusted with herself, she thought she would take the sandy track by the lime kiln and not the gravelled lane. The whiteness of the lime shells baking in the heat of the husk forming in her memory, she walked along the kiln, built like a well with hard clay and exposed bricks, laden with ash and charcoal. Thinking of the scattered particles flying out of its cracked-up, blackened chimney, she stood in front of the kiln. The scent of the smouldering shells settling heavily on her, she started running down from the tarred road towards the sandy track, along the fence of the lime kiln, made of dried palm leaves.

She felt she needed to walk under the cashew trees to avoid the sweltering heat. She walked thinking that the branches of the cashew trees curled up like creepers, were sprawled on the white sand like a caved-in green tent. She realized her exhaustion, with the burning sun hitting her straight in the face, walking on that aimless, meandering track, lined with cactus and scrubs, some with thick leaves and some full of thorns. Once again her headache began to show its presence. She felt the piece of shrapnel inside her head on the left side heating up and its heat spreading across her face. She walked faster, realizing that her feet burnt sharply as her flat slippers sank into the sand.

She felt an obscure hope looking at the green, budding leaves on top of the palm-like drumstick tree, planted along the ridges of the sand-bunds to firm them, shoring up the abandoned betel field, almost to half as high as a coconut tree. Bending forward, she climbed up the slope of the crumbled sand-bund, as if looking for her father's hopes and drops of sweat. She felt irritated at the grains of sand caught between the slippers and her feet that were thrown up, hitting her neck, getting into her shirt, sticking to the sweat, and rubbing her.

Standing with one leg on the ridge of the sand-bund and the other on its slope, she turned to look back as if something that she lost a long time ago was lying there somewhere behind her. She felt as if the pond, thick with black algae and grass, with little water, had moved far from the sand-bund on which she was standing. She remembered when her father had his betel field on this sand-bund, the pond was bigger, with more water, closer to the field's fence; its memory sprouted afresh and dissolved in her mind. Her father's dark, emaciated body, just a piece of cloth around him, carrying water in a large earthen pot from the pond, climbing on to the sand-bund with his feet sinking into sand, appeared in her mind as an image on the water in the pond, only to dissolve like water bubbles, swept away by waves. She saw a hazy image taking shape in the mirage from the scorching sand, with sirissa trunks chopped for wood, of her brother and her, peeling and eating tapioca, roasted under the sirissa tree with its hanging, long, green pods, still feeling the tapioca's warmth in their hands. She stood staggering, as if the green betel vines—which were her food, which were her books—were spitting out fiery wind at her, unsettling her as they swayed. She felt as if her legs were buckling, losing strength, like her left arm, when she remembered that this is the field her father had toiled on, carrying earth in baskets, mixed with sand, dung and sweat, and planting vines.

She came to the centre of the scorching sand-bund, letting her gaze wander in the direction of the settlements in the distance. She saw the scattered, squat houses of stone and their red tiles, with the names of organizations engraved in white on them, through the thick faded leaves of the cashew branches, scrubs and white sand dunes. She saw that the cone-shaped huts made of tin sheets and palm leaves have disappeared completely, as she had seen them when she left to join the movement. She looked sharply at her own hut, forcing her gaze through the sweeping waves of the broiling wind. She ensured that the tiled house, built by organizations, standing mutely next to the tall, white tent, with UNICEF embossed with blue paint on it, was theirs. She sharpened her gaze further, despite the heat. She felt her eyes taking in people, appearing taller than the sloped roof of her house, clad in white clothes, walking around inside the tent and outside her house. She saw hazy faces of relatives amidst the vivid moments of hurried preparations for a cremation, swaying in her memory, inside her tearful eyes.

She thought about the moments when she was leaving, not sure whether to feel happy or sad that it was the news of her younger brother's death, conveyed by the Red Cross, which turned into the reason for her own release.

'He seems to have fallen in love with some education officer's daughter in the campus. That girl's father seems to have slapped him in front of the others in the campus . . . the same night he hanged himself from a tree . . . we will try to keep the body for three days . . . if they let you go, come and see his face for the last time.'

Uncle Govindan, who had come along with the Red Cross, informed her.

She remembered the betel-chewing mouth and the stained clothes of the old man, who served food at the camp, who like her own father had showered pure affection on her, had signed the bond and helped her board the bus.

Remembering the screaming sounds coming out of the loudspeaker, she felt her eardums were slammed, as the leader spoke constantly at public events and school sports competitions, and said, 'Boy or girl . . . one from each family must come to fight.'

'The boy is very smart . . . intelligent . . . He will join the campus somehow . . . if he makes it, he will carry the family ashore.'

When Uncle Govindan repeated this, she reminded herself of how her father kept listening to him, oblivious of its intent. She recalled the moments of that night, and the bright sandy tracks shining in the moonlight, as she left to join the movement in the middle of the night, leaving a letter for the sake of her brother and her family.

In the sweltering heat, as the piece of the 'shell', still inside her head, gained heat, she felt her head and body simmering along with her nerves and veins. She got down from the sand dune, and gathering her senses, walked in the direction of her house. She could feel herself beginning to digest the sounds of wailing, lamenting and the commands of rituals, well before she neared her house.

When she started to listen to the rustling conversations and lamentations closely, she felt the thorny bushes and the eecham shrubs were the only ones screening her from revealing herself. She suddenly felt the stench of sulphur in the air. She felt fear, as a single Chinese cracker that burst nearby, vibrated and subsided inside her head. She heard the subsiding echo of the cracker against the sky like clothes beaten and washed on stone.

In the rush to present herself, her legs fumbled and, losing all control, she saw the thorny scrubs and the hot sand, closing in fast, straight on her face. Realizing that she could not use her lame left arm, she jerked her body rightwards, and her right shoulder hitting the ground hard, she fell with her head striking the hot sand. Once again the stench of sulphur hit her; she heard the bursting sounds of bundles of crackers very close by. Scattered shards of paper and sparks of fire kept appearing suddenly.

She felt the stiffness and pain, as if countless number of needles were piercing inside her head, along with sounds and echoes of constant bursts. As the pain grew, she felt hapless, unable to control her legs shivering, then trembling on the hot sand. She heard her teeth grinding as her jaws stiffened. Her eyes darkened when her entire body shrunk, shivered and began to tremble.

She felt the continuous sounds and echoes of the Chinese crackers inside her ears; they were turning gradually into sounds of bursting gunshots, without echoes. She felt a shapeless memory rising in her mind, of her shooting incessantly, despite feeling the searing heat of not just the steel parts of her gun but also its wooden parts. What stayed in her mind was the memory of the pain she felt when heavily wounded by the flying splinters of stone, bursting out of the concrete bunker, as a bullet from the other side smashed into it. She sensed the discontinuous, intermittent, fierce stench of the charred concrete bunker, smashed by the bullet, assailing her nose hard, and unsettling her. She tried to bring to her mind that scene of the torrent of light that appeared like a lightning strike, as she was shooting continuously. She only recollected how she felt when the strong, massive, silent heap of sand, moved towards the bunker. After a thundering sound and a sandstorm had passed, she saw the bunker shrouded in heaps of sand and ruined branches of trees, which appeared in her memory like images of violent scenes in a movie, shown in negative. As she felt the fresh hot blood spreading from the left side of the head down to her cheeks and from the place where her two fingers appeared to have been spliced by a sharp blade, the roaring noise inside her ears stopped and she completely lost her consciousness.

She felt her senses coming back, along with the left-side headache. She felt her body lying soaked in sweat, as if drenched in rain. She thought her sweat made the sand and the churidhar, bought by someone else, which she was wearing, stick together oppressively, making her feel disgusted. She could feel the persistent dizziness inside her head as she opened her eyes. She was shocked when she realized that the sky had turned ashen and dusk was setting in. She thought, she felt sad as her senses made her aware of the complete silence of the dead house. She could feel her body absorbing the latent heat of the sand, still hot from the day. Clamping her teeth, she could feel the pain in her jaws and the salt in her lips.

Getting up, stepping across the thorny scrubs and the eecham shrubs that were like a screen blocking her, she saw her father stooped, innocently in front of some relatives. She stood there drained, with the rush of implacable emotions egging her on to get back and sit behind the screen of the thorny scrubs and eecham shrubs, until dark, hiding her left arm with the white dupatta. Salvaging the memories of she and her brother watering the greens and eating smoked cashewnuts together, she went back, sitting behind the screen of the thorny scrub and the eecham shrubs, and wilted into tears.

Translated by D. Senthil Babu

V. Gowribalan, '*Thirumputal*' (2014). Unpublished in Tamil.

Note on Authors

Mahakavi (1927–1971)
Thu. Uruthiramurthy was from Jaffna and worked as a government official. He is acclaimed for having introduced novel forms and patterns in modern Tamil poetry of Sri Lanka. As a versatile author, he wrote several lyrical plays, poetry and short stories. He also edited a journal of poetry, *Thenmozhi*, published just for a year in 1955–56.

Dominic Jeeva (1927–)
Left-leaning, politically, Dominic Jeeva is from Jaffna. He is a Dalit and a hairdresser by profession. His shop was known as a hub for writers and poets. He founded the literary journal *Mallikai* in the 1960s, which continues to be published to this day. Presently, he lives in Colombo and has published several collections of his short stories, besides his autobiography.

Mu. Thalaiyasingam (1935–1973)
Mu. Thalaiyasingam was from Pungudu Island in Jaffna. A school teacher by profession, he was also a reformist active in anti-caste struggles and a philosopher steeped in spiritual and non-violent modes of resistance, inspired by Mahatma Gandhi. To him, literature was integral to the pursuit of a new humanism. He was the first among his generation to conceive of a Tamil homeland in Sri Lanka. He has authored works in philosophy and has written short stories and a novel.

Neelavanan (1931–1975)
K. Chinnathurai, a school teacher, was from Periya Neelavanai in Eastern Sri Lanka, who assumed the pen name of Neelavanan after

the name of his village. Along with many poems, he wrote lyrical plays. He was the president of the Writers Association based in Kalmunai in Eastern Sri Lanka. He also edited a literary journal, *Paadum Meen.*

Mu. Ponnampalam (1939–)
Mu. Ponnampalam, the younger brother of Mu. Thalaiyasingam, is from Pungudu island in Jaffna. He is known for his novel, *Noyil Iruthal*. He lives in Colombo.

M.A. Nuhman (1944–)
M.A. Nuhman is from Kalmunaikudi in Eastern Sri Lanka. He pursued research in linguistics and became a professor of Tamil at the University of Peradeniya, Sri Lanka. He is well known as a critic and a translator. His translation of poetry from Palestine (1981) in Tamil and his anthology of Ealam Tamil poetry (1984) are considered landmarks in Sri Lankan Tamil literature.

A. Jesurasa (1946–)
A. Jesurasa is from Kurunagar village in Jaffna. He worked as a postmaster. He was one of the editors of *Alai,* an important modern literary journal, in the late 1970s. He is an avid film enthusiast and critic. He also edited the anthology of Ealam Tamil poetry of 1984 along with M.A. Nuhman. He lives in Jaffna.

S. Sivasegaram (1942–)
S. Sivasegaram, from Inuvil village in Jaffna, is an engineer by training. He was professor of mechanical engineering in the University of Peradeniya. A Marxist, he has published many volumes of poetry. He is also a translator.

V.I.S. Jayapalan (1944–)
V.I.S. Jayapalan is from Neduntheevu village in Jaffna. A graduate in economics, he is well known as a poet and essayist. He has published many collections of his poetry. Since the 1970s he has been living in Norway. He has also acted in popular Tamil movies.

Shanmugam Sivalingam (1940–2012)
A graduate teacher in science, Shanmugam Sivalingam hailed from Pandi Iruppu village in Eastern Sri Lanka. He was not a prolific poet and published just two poetry collections in his lifetime. He also wrote short stories. One of his sons was a militant and was killed in war.

Piramil (1939–1997)
Piramil was from Triconamalai, Sri Lanka. He was known by various pen names which he formulated from his practice of numerology. Even after migrating to India in the 1970s, he remained a Sri Lankan Tamil at heart. He firmly stood for a unified Sri Lankan country with a fusion of both Sinhalese and Tamil cultural traditions. He is considered a major poet in contemporary Tamil. He has also written short stories and plays.

Sivaramani (1968–1991)
Sivaramani, whose parents were teachers, came from Yaanaippanthi village, Jaffna. She studied English literature, political science and linguistics at the University of Jaffna. Along with her friends, she founded the Women's Study Circle in Jaffna. She was active during her university student life in resistance against the fraught political environment of the late 1980s. She committed suicide in 1991. Her collection of poems was published posthumously.

Su. Vilvarathinam (1950–2006)

Su. Vilvarathinam, from Pungudi island in Jaffna, was a government official. He regarded Thalaiyasingam as his mentor and was active in anti-caste struggles. A powerful poet, he stood for spiritual values, yet was rebellious. Considered as the lyrical poet par excellence of his generation, he was a very good singer and orator.

S. Ranjakumar (1959–)

Somabala Ranjakumar is from Karaveddi, Jaffna. His only collection of short stories, *Mogavasal*, was written and published in 1989. This collection is considered to be highly significant, one that captured the deep anxieties of the Tamil people after the riots of 1983, known as Black July. He worked in a printing press and lived between Jaffna and Colombo. He now lives in Australia.

Aswagosh (1969–)

Ramanaiah Kathiravel, from Navindil, Karaveddi, in Jaffna, wrote in the name of Puthiya Jeevan till the nineties. Afterwards he assumed the name of Aswagosh. He has so far published two poetry collections, in 1997 and 1999. He has also written essays in the name of Ram Kathiravel. He lives in Colombo.

Ilavalai Wijayendran (1961–)

Wijayendran Thiyagaraja is from Nurelia (Nuwara Eliya), near Kandy, in the hill country. He has been a journalist in Sri Lanka. He moved to Norway, from where he edited a literary journal, *Suvadugal*.

Pa. Ahilan (1970–)

Pakkianathan Ahilan, from Jaffna, is a postgraduate in fine arts from MS University, Baroda, India. He teaches art history in the University of Jaffna. He has published two poetry collections, in 2001 and 2011.

Malaravan (1972–1992)
Known by his *noms de guerre* Captain Malaravan and Leo, Kasilingam Vijeethan was from Thirunelveli, Jaffna. He served in the army of the LTTE and was killed in combat in 1992. He was a gifted narrator, sensitive to the human context in the zone of war, despite being a shrewd military analyst. He is primarily known for his war diary, *Por Ula* (1993). He has also written a novel, *Puyal Paravai*, that was posthumously published in 2003 in Killinocchi.

Cheran (1958–)
Son of the poet Mahakavi, Cheran belongs to Alavetty, Jaffna. He teaches in the Department of Sociology and Anthropology at the University of Windsor, Canada. *Maranathul Vaazhvom*, an anthology of Sri Lankan Tamil poetry that he coedited in 1985, is considered to be a significant collection.

Maalika (1948–?)
Maalika was reportedly the pen name of Puthuvai Rathinadurai, from Puthur village in Jaffna. A dynamic and popular lyrical poet, he headed the Arts and Culture Wing of the LTTE; his poems and songs were the mainstay of their propaganda. He surrendered to the Sri Lankan Army in May 2009, after the war. Nothing has been known about him since. The Sri Lankan authorities refuse to entertain any queries about him.

Majeed (1969–)
Adam Kandu Abdul Majeed is from Akkaraippatru, Ambarai, in Eastern Sri Lanka. He has published two poetry collections. He lives in Akkaraippatru and works as an assistant librarian.

Muralisvaran (1976–)
Dr Rarasarathnam Muralisvaran, from Nelliyadi village in Jaffna, studied medicine in the Jaffna Medical College. He practises in

Batticaloa. His collection of poems will be published towards the end of this year.

Bose Nilhale (1975–2007)
Chandrabose Sudhakar was from Palai near Killinocchi. He worked as a journalist. Known to be self-righteous to the point of being uncompromising, he was killed by unknown assailants in front of his family, in Vavuniya. He edited and published a literary journal, *Nilam*. His poems and writings will be published as a book for the first time by the end of 2014.

Rashmy (1974–)
A painter and book designer, Ahamed Rashmy Mohamed is from Akkaraippatru in Eastern Sri Lanka. He now lives in the UK, where he works as a journalist. He has published four poetry collections.

Selvam Arulanantham (1953–)
Selvam Arulanantham is from Sillalai, Jaffna. He edits a literary journal, *Kaalam*, published from Toronto, where he now lives. He is pivotal to the circulation of Tamil literature in the Tamil Diaspora of Canada.

Aruntati (1957–)
Arulananda Raja is from Naavanthurai, Jaffna. He moved to Paris in 1984. In 1996, he made a Tamil feature film, *Mugam*. He has published two poetry collections and is also a playwright and director.

Nilanthan (1965–)
Nilanthan is from Jaffna. Due to the war, he moved to Vanni in 1995. He lived in the war zone till 2009. Now he lives in Jaffna, where he works as a private English tutor. He is a painter, who has also written plays and political essays.

Kumarmurthy (1956–2001)
Kumarasamy Vinayagamurthy is from Delft (Neduntheevu), Jaffna. He grew up in Thambanai in the Vanni region. For a while, he worked on a ship. He was politically active for some time with the People's Liberation Organization of Tamil Ealam (PLOTE). He moved to Canada in 1986 and was a human rights activist. He has published two short story collections.

Iravi Arunasalam (1960–)
A graduate in Tamil with a diploma in education, A. Ravi is from Alavetty, Jaffna. He worked as a schoolteacher in Sri Lanka before he moved to Europe, where he works as a journalist. He now lives in London. He has published two memoirs and a collection of his short stories.

Karunakaran (1963–)
Karunakaran, also known as Vasantharajan, from Iyackachi, Northern Sri Lanka, shifted to Vanni in 1995 due to the compulsions of the war. After the war, he moved to Jaffna, where he lives now. He was the editor of an important literary journal, *Velicham*, published from Vanni during the war years. He has published four collections of poetry and one of short stories.

V. Gowribalan (1970–)
V. Gowribalan is from Uppuveli, Triconamalai. Trained as a draughtsman, he shifted to Jaffna in 1989. He now lives in Batticaloa. He is a management assistant in the government. His short story collection *Oppanai Nizhal* (2003) is a stark portrayal of the grim realities of the marginalized during the war years.

Ilaiya Abdullah (1968–)
M.N.M. Anas is from Mullaittivu, Northern Sri Lanka. He works as a journalist and has been writing since 1985. He has published

two poetry collections, one short story collection and another one of essays. He works for a Tamil TV channel in London.

S. Vinodhine (1969–)
Vinodhine Sachidanandan, from Thellippalai, Jaffna, started writing in the 1980s, both in English and Tamil. She has published one poetry collection, and lives in the USA.

Faheema Jahan (1973–)
A mathematics teacher, Faheema Jahan is from Melsiripuram in Kurunagal district, North-western Sri Lanka. She has published three poetry collections.

S. Chelian (1960–)
S. Sivakumaran, from Urumpirai, Jaffna, became involved in the Tamil liberation struggle at an early age. He left Sri Lanka in 1986 as a refugee and has been living in Canada ever since. He has written short stories and plays, and has five collections of poems.

T. Malar Chelvan (1968–)
T. Malar Chelvan, who works in the department of culture in Catticaloa in Eastern Sri Lanka, comes from Aaraiyampathi in the same area. He has published a collection each of poetry and short stories. Since 2003, he edits a literary journal, *Maruka*.

Deebachelvan (1983–)
Balendran Pradipan is from Rathinapuram, Killinocchi district, northern Sri Lanka. He is a postgraduate in journalism and media, and works as a journalist and a photographer. He has published five collections of his poetry, three of his essays and a memoir.

Tha. Agilan (1983–)
Agilan Thadchanamoorthy is a journalist and photographer from Killinocchi, Northern Sri Lanka. He has published a collection of his poems and a memoir. He lives in Canada where he runs a publishing house, Vadali, that specializes in bringing out rare and out-of-print works from Sri Lankan Tamil literature.

Ki. Pi. Aravinthan (1953–)
Christopher Francis, belonging to Jaffna, was involved in the liberation struggle during its early years. He moved to Paris in 1991 from where he edited a literary journal, *Mounam*, for many years. He has published three poetry collections. Recently, his poetry has been translated into French.

Na. Sathyabalan (1956–)
Nataraja Sathyabalan is from Nallur, Jaffna. He is an English teacher. He has published a poetry collection.

Malliyappu Santhi Thilagar (1973–)
Mylvaganam Thilakarajah, a Sri Lankan-Indian-origin upcountry Tamil, comes from North Medacombara (Tea) Estate, Watagoda, Sri Lanka. He studied management in the University of Colombo and works as a management consultant in a private firm. He has published a collection of his poems.

Acknowledgements

This anthology was made possible by our friends, the Sri Lankan Tamil writers, who generously allowed us to translate and publish their works. In particular, we would like to thank V. Gowribalan, Pathmanabhan Iyer, Shobhasakthi, Tha. Agilan, Pa. Ahilan, Karunakaran, Nilanthan and Paramasothi Senavarayar. We thank Professor George Hart, Kiran Keshavamurthy and N. Malathy for allowing us to use their translations in this book.

At the French Institute of Pondicherry, we thank its Director, Pierre Grard, its Secretary General, Eve Herrman, and our colleagues and friends: G. Muthushankar, Anurupa Naik, R. Narendiran, K. Ramanujam, G. Saravanan, V. Prakash, P. Balamurugan, S. Prabhavathi, A. Pankajavalli and Vanitha Bruno for all their support and encouragement. This project would not have been possible without the full-fledged support of the French Institute of Pondicherry and its resources.

Professor Francois Gros, Professor Y. Subbarayalu and Mr Eric Whittington remained committed to the fulfilment of this project right from its beginning, and we hope it meets their expectations.

Kamini Mahadevan, our editor at Penguin, made this project possible. We were fortunate to work with her closely, making it for us an enjoyable learning experience.

One of us, Rebecca Whittington, would like to thank her friend Shamila Sivakumaran and Professors George and Kausalya Hart and Chana Kronfeld at the University of California, Berkeley. She would also like to thank her husband Abhijeet, who has learnt one word in Tamil very well—*anputan*. And last but not least, her daughter Kuheli, or Monima, known in Tamil as Kuyili, or Muniyamma, who is known to thumb through the Tamil dictionary with great concentration, looking for the picture of the dog.

We thank our friend Maragadamme Sitharamane for being there in those times of translation.

We thank Anupama Krishnamurthy, Varalakshmi Krishnamurthy, Manimekalai Dhandapani, Balasubramanian and Egile Tiroutchelvy for sustaining us and making us go on.

Two of us, Kannan M. and Senthil Babu, would like to thank our nieces, Ria, Sahana, Vedha, Nivanthi and Niyantha just for being with us and 'performing the delightful miracle of remaining children while seeing the world through our eyes'.

Copyright Acknowledgements

Grateful acknowledgement is made to the following for permission to reprint copyright material:

A. Jesurasa: A. Jesurasa for '*Unnudaiyavum Kathi*', in M.A. Nuhman and A. Jesurasa (eds), *Patinoru Eelattu Kavingargal*, CreA, Chennai, 1984, p. 179.

Aruntati: Aruntati for '*Kelvigal*' (1999); first appeared *in Uyir Nizhal Journal*, Paris, March–April 1999; published in Sugan (ed.), *Theendathagaathavan Muthalaana Eelathu Dalit Sirukathaigal 14*, Maalika Books, Chennai, 2007, pp. 128–141.

Aswagosh: Aswagosh for '*Irul*' (1990), in *Vanathin Azhaippu*, Nigari, Kalkilai, 1997, pp. 16–18.

Bose Nilhale: Son of Bose Nihale for '*Veenai*' (1999), in *Sarinigar*, No. 172 (27 May–9 June 1999, Colombo; published in *Vetraaki Ninra Veli*, Vitiyal, Coimbatore, 2001, p. 23; for '*Nigazh*', in *Sarinigar*, No. 172, 27 May–9 June 1999, Colombo; published in *Vetraagi Ninra Veli*, Vitiyal, Coimbatore, 2001, p. 22.

Chelian: Chelian for '*Chinnathambi*' (2010), *Kaalam* Journal, January–March 2010; for '*Karunaiyum Illadavargal*', in *Kadalai Vittuppona Meen Kunjugal*, Kaalam, Toronto, 2007, p. 16.

Cheran: Cheran for '*Veerargal Thuyilum Nilam*', in *Sarinigar*, No. 172, 27 May–9 June 1995, Colombo; published in *Vetraagi Ninra Veli*, Vitiyal, Coimbatore, 2001, pp. 15–17.

Deebachelvan: Deebachelvan for '*Nilam Peyarnthalaiya Vandhu Vidu*' (April–May 2009), in *Aatkaltra Nagarathai Thinra Mirugam*, Uyirmai, Chennai, 2009, pp. 91–92.

Dominic Jeeva: Dominic Jeeva for '*Gnanam*' (around the early 1960s), in *Dominic Jeeva Sirukataikal*, Mallikaippantal, Jaffna, 1996, pp. 109–118

Faheema Jahan: Faheema Jahan for '*Azhivin Pinnar*', in *Oru Katal Nirurril*, Panikkudam, Chennai, 2007, p. 12; for '*Enathu Kaimarri Yenthi Kol*', in *Abarathi*, Vadali, Chennai, 2009, pp. 17–18.

Ilaiya Abdullah: Ilaiya Abdullah for '*Ethirkollal*', in *Pinam Seyyum Desam*, Uyirmai, Chennai, 2004.

Ilavalai Wijayendran: Ilavalai Wijayendran for '*Thadi Kondu Tiribavargalukku*' (1990), in *Niramarru Pona Kanavugal*, Desiya Kalai Ilakkiya Peravai and South Vision, Colombo, Chennai, 1999, p. 56.

Iravi Arunasalam: Iravi Arunasalam for '*Kaalam Aki Vanta Katai*', in *Kaalam Aki Vanta Katai*, Vitiyal, Coimbatore, 2003, pp. 21–25.

Ki. Pi. Aravinthan: Ki. Pi. Aravinthan for '*Oru Agathiyin Thaayum Thayagamum*' (2004), in *Iruppum Veruppum*, Salaram, Chennai, 2009, pp. 100–109; for '*Kadalum Kanavum*' (2012), *Kakkai Cirakinile* Journal, May 2012, Chennai, p. 3.

Karunakaran: Karunakaran for '*Varugaialaridam Sila Kelvi*', in *Oru Payaniyin Nigazhkala Kurippugal*, Magizh, Putu Kudiyuruppu, 2003, p. 36; for '*Thagikkum Koodu*' (2009), in *Pali Aadu*, Vadali, Chennai, 2009, p. 30; for '*Karuppu Nai*' (2009), in ibid., p. 85; for '*Nizhalai Vilakka Mudiyaatha Por Veeran*' (2009), in ibid., pp. 97–98; for '*Oyaa Kadal . . . Urangaa Nilam . . . Theeraa Kanavu*' (2011), in Karunakaran, *Oru Payaniyin Porkala Kurippugal*, Karrupu Pirathigal, Chennai, 2012, pp. 90–91; for '*Neeye Vaiththiru Avarraiyellam*', in ibid., p. 30.

Kumaramurthy: Son of Kumaramurthy for '*Hanifavum Irandu Erudugalum*', in *Kumaramurthy Kathaigal*, Kaalam, Toronto, 2002, pp. 29–35.

M.A. Nuhman: M.A. Nuhman for *'Nerraiya Malaiyum Inraiya Kaalaiyum'*, in *Alai* Journal, Jaffna, December 1977, pp. 239–240.

Maalika*: Maalika for *'Oriravil'*, in *Erimalai*, September 1996; published in *Vetraagi Ninra Veli*, Vitiyal, Coimbatore, 2001, p. 47.

Mahakavi: The estate of Mahakavi and Cheran for *Therum Thingalum*, in M.A. Nuhman and A. Yesurasa (eds), *Patinoru Eelattu Kavingargal*, CreA, Chennai, 1984, pp. 27–28.

Majeed: Majeed for *'Ulmana Veli Parappinil'*, in *Sarinigar*, No. 162, 24 December–14 January 1998, Colombo; published in *Vetraaki Ninra Veli*, Vitiyal, Coimbatore, 2001, p. 25; for *'Ner Kottu Parappalave Enakkullum Thuyar'* (1998), in *Sarinigar*, No. 152, 6–10 August 1998, Colombo; published in *Vetraaki Ninra Veli*, Vitiyal, Coimbatore, 2001, p. 26.

Malaravan: N. Malathy for extract from *War Journey: Diary of a Tamil Tiger*, translated by N. Malathy, Penguin Books India, New Delhi, 2013, pp. 59–73; *Por Ula*, Publication Division, LTTE, Killinocchi, 1993; second edition, Vitiyal, Coimbatore, 2009.

Malliappu Santhi Thilagar: Malliappu Santhi Thilagar for *'Yaazhppanathil Madakkombarai'*, in *Jeevanathi*, No. 63, December 2013, pp. 39–47. Published from Nelliady, Jaffna.

Mu. Ponnampalam: Mu. Ponnampalam for *'Natai'*, in Mu. Ponnampalam, *Kaalil Leelai*, Dhwani, Chennai, 1997, pp. 90–91.

Mu. Thalaiyasingam: The estate of Thalaiyasingam for *'Sree La Sree Arumuga Naavalarku Ezhudhum Vinnappam'*, in Mu. Ponnampalam (ed.), *Thalayasinkam Padaippukal*, Kalachuvadu, Nagerkovil, 2006, pp. 771–783.

---

* Maalika was reportedly one of the pen names used by the poet Pudhuvai Rathinadurai.

Na. Sathyabalan: Na. Sathyabalan for '*Ezhudhappadaadha Madalonrin Kathai*' (2010), in http://marupaathy.blogspot.in/2010/09/blog-post_2958.html

Neelavanan: Son of Neelavanan for '*O . . . O . . . Vandikkara*', in M.A. Nuhman and A. Jesurasa (eds), *Patinoru Eelattu Kavingargal*, CreA, Chennai, 1984, p. 81.

Nilathan: Nilanthan for extracts from two long poems, '*Vannimaanmiyam*' and '*Yaazhppaaname, Enathu Yaazhppaaname!*' by Nilanthan; '*Vannimaanmiyam*' first appeared in *Niyathi*, Mallaavi, 2002; '*Yaazhppaaname, Enathu Yaazhppaaname!*' first appeared in *Magizh*, Puthu Kudiyuruppu, 2002. These poems are published in Nilanthan, *Ini Enathu Naatkale Varum*, Vitiyal, Coimbatore, 2012; for '*Yugappuranam*' (2011), in *Ini Enathu Naatkale Varum*, Vitiyal, Coimbatore, 2012, pp. 93–99.

Pa. Ahilan: Pa. Ahilan for '*Pathungu Kuzhi Natkal*' (1992), in *Pathungu Kuzhi Natkal*, Kuruthu, Erode, 2000, p. 15; Pa. Ahilan, '*Peru Nilam—Mannadukkugal Parriya Arimugam*' (2010), in *Saramakavigal*, Peru, Jaffna, 2011, p. 45.

Piramil: Estate of Piramil for '*Lankapuri Raja*' (23 June 1985), in *Tinamani Katir*, Chennai; in K. Subramaniam (ed.), *Piramil Pataippukal*, Adaiyalam, Puthanatham, 2003, pp. 101–111.

R. Muralisvaran: R. Muralisvaran for '*Tholaintha Vaazhvu*', in *Sarinigar*, No. 155, 17–30 September 1998, Colombo; published in *Vetraaki Ninra Veli*, Vitiyal, Coimbatore, 2001, 29–30.

Ranjakumar: Ranjakumar for '*Kaalam Unakku Oru Paattu Ezhudum*', in Ranjakumar, *Mokavasal*, Yathartha, Paruthithurai, 1989, pp. 18–31.

Rashmy: Rashmy for '*Eemam*' (1999), in *Kaavu Kollappatta Vaazhvu Mudalaaya Kavithaigal*, Exil, Coubevoie, 2002, pp. 49–51.

S. Sivasegaram: S. Sivasegaram for '*Payanam*', in M.A. Nuhman and A. Jesurasa (eds), *Patinoru Eelattu Kavingargal*, CreA, Chennai, 1984, p. 170.

Selvam Arulanantham: Selvam Arulanantham for '*Vyakula Prasangam*', in *Thotruthaan Povoma*, Sabalingam Nanbargal Vattam, Gorges Les Gonesse, France, 1999; published in *Vetraagi Ninra Veli*, Vitiyal, Coimbatore, 2001, p. 50.

Shanmugam Sivalingam: Estate of Shanmugam Sivalingam for '*Paadatha Padalkal*', in Shanmugam Sivalingam, *Neer Valaiyangal*, Tamizhiyal, Chennai, 1988, pp. 112–113; for '*Sithaninthu Pona Desamum Thoornthu Pone Manakkugaiyum*' (1997), in *Kalachuvadu*, Tamiliyal, Nagerkovil, 2010, pp. 195–196; for '*Oru Sarvadesa Agatiyin Paadal*' (1990), in *Sithaninthu Pona Desamum Thoornthu Pone Manakkugaiyum, Kalachuvadu*, Tamiliyal, Nagerkovil, 2010, pp. 205–206.

Sivaramani: Sivaramani for '*Maalai Nerangalil*' (1989), in *Sivaramani Kavithaigal*, Women's Study Circle, Batticaloa, 1993, pp. 39–41; for '*Ennidam*'(1989), in ibid., p. 38; for '*Enathu Paramparaiyum Naanum*' (1989), in ibid., pp. 42–43; for '*Thanithu*' (1989), in ibid., p. 46–47; for '*Avamaana Paduthappattaval*' (1990), in ibid, p. 44–45.

Su. Vilvarathinam: Su. Vilvarathinam's estate for *Oru Paalaiyin Kural* (1989), in *Uyirtthezhum Kaalathirkaga*, Vitiyal, Coimbatore, 2001, pp. 157–158; for '*Vetraki Ninra Veli*' (1994), in ibid., pp. 139–140; for '*Nilavin Ethiroli*' (1999), in ibid., pp. 324–325.

T. Malar Chelvan: T. Malar Chelvan for '*Anji Maraikkal Pallan*', in *Uyir Nizhal*, January–July 2009, Paris, p. 58.

Tha. Agilan: Tha. Agilan for '*Oru Paiyanin Appa Irandu Ponar*', in *Maranathin Vaasanai*, E. Pathippagam, Chennai, 2009, pp. 21–27.

V. Gowribalan: V. Gowribalan for '*Appe Ratta*' (2003), in *Oppanai Nizhal* (first edition 2003), Parisal, Chennai, 2010, pp. 89–96; for '*Irumbu*

Paravaigal', in *Oppanai Nizhal* (first edition 2003), Parisal, Chennai, 2010, pp. 56–63; for '*Thirumputal*' (2014). Unpublished in Tamil.

V.I.S. Jayapalan: V.I.S. Jayapalan for '*Nambikkai*', in M.A. Nuhman and A. Jesurasa (eds), *Patinoru Eelattu Kavingargal*, CreA, Chennai, 1984, p. 186; for '*Kadarpuram*', in M.A. Nuhman and A. Jesurasa, ibid., p. 190; for '*Ettavathu Pey*' (1997), in *Sarinigar*, No. 135, 20 November–3 December 1997, Colombo; published in *Vetraagi Ninra Veli*, Vitiyal, Coimbatore, 2001, pp. 41–42.

Vinodhine: Vinodhine for '*Iravu*' (2004), in *Mugamoodi Seibaval*, Kalachuvadu, Nagerkovil, 2007, p. 28; for '*Nedum Pagal*' (2006), in ibid., p. 39; for '*Enadhu Paadalgalai Naan*', in ibid., p. 76; for '*Avargalai Konravargal*', in ibid., p. 30.

Further Reading

The selection below, listed in the chronological order, is intended to orient the reader to the particular contexts in which Sri Lankan Tamil literature emerged. We have confined ourselves to works available in English related to the writings in this anthology and their period. We have also given a list of translations of Sri Lankan Tamil literature, which are already available in print. The sources available in Tamil, including those available online, are too numerous to be listed here.

The Background

Balasingham, Adele. *The Will to Freedom: An Inside View of Tamil Resistance*. Mitcham: Fairmax Publishing, 2011.

Balasingham, Anton. *War and Peace: Armed Struggle and Peace Efforts of Liberation Tigers*. Mitcham: Fairmax Publishing, 2004.

Bass, Daniel. *Everyday Ethnicity in Sri Lanka: Up-country Tamil Identity Politics*. Abingdon, Oxon: Routledge, 2013.

Daniel, E. Valentine. *Chapters in an Anthropography of Violence: Sri Lankans, Sinhalas and Tamils*. New Delhi: Oxford University Press, New Delhi, 1997.

David, S.A. *Tamil Ealam Freedom Struggle*. Chennai: World Tamil Reader's Trust, 2004.

de Soyza, Niromi. *Tamil Tigress: My Story as a Child Soldier in Sri Lanka's Bloody Civil War*. Sydney: Allen & Unwin, 2011; Pune: Mehta Publishing House, 2012.

Gunawardana, R.A.L.H. 'The People of the Lion: Sinhala Identity and Ideology in History and Historiography'. In *Sri Lanka and the Roots of Conflict*, edited by Jonathan Spencer, pp. 70–78. London: Routledge, 1990.

———. *Historiography in a Time of Ethnic Conflict—Construction of the Past in Contemporary Sri Lanka*. Colombo: Social Scientist Association, 1995.

Harrison, Frances. *Still Counting the Dead: Survivors of Sri Lanka's Hidden War*. London: Portobello Books, 2012.

Indrapala, K. *The Evolution of an Ethnic Identity: The Tamils in Sri Lanka, c. 300 BCE to c. 1200 CE*. Sydney: MV Publications, South Asian Study Centre. (Indian edition, Colombo and Chennai: Kumaran Book House, 2006.)

Kanapathipillai, Valli. *Citizenship and Statelessness in Sri Lanka: The Case of the Tamil Estate Workers*. Anthem South Asian Studies. London, New Delhi: Anthem Press, 2012. (First edition, UK, US, 2009.)

Manivannan, Ramu. *Sri Lanka: Hiding the Elephant—Documenting Genocide, War Crimes and Crimes Against Humanity*. Chennai: Department of Politics and Public Administration, University of Madras, 2014.

Malathy, N. *A Fleeting Moment in My Country: The Last Years of the LTTE De-Facto State*. Atlanta: Clarity Press, 2012; New Delhi: Aakar Books, 2012.)

McGilvray, Dennis B. *Symbolic Heat: Gender, Health and Worship among the Tamils of South India and Sri Lanka*. Boulder: Mapin Publications in association with University of Colorado Museum, 1998.

———. *Crucible of Conflict: Tamil and Muslim Society on the East Coast of Sri Lanka*. Durham: Duke University Press, 2008.

McGilvray, Dennis B. and Mirak Raheem. *Muslim Perspectives on the Sri Lankan Conflict*. Washington: East-West Center, 2007.

McGowan, William. *Only Man Is Vile: The Tragedy of Sri Lanka*. New York: Farrar, Straus and Giroux, 1992.

Mohan, Rohini. *The Seasons of Trouble: Life Amid the Ruins of Sri Lanka's War*. London: Verso Books, 2014.

Moldrich, Donovan. *Bitter Berry Bondage: The Nineteenth Century Coffee Workers of Sri Lanka*. Kandy: Coordinating Secretariat for Plantation Areas, 1989.

Nadesan, S. *A History of the Up-Country Tamil People in Sri Lanka*. Hatton: Nandalala Publication, 1993.

Nuhman, M.A. *Sri Lankan Muslims: Ethnic Identity within Cultural Diversity*. Colombo: International Centre for Ethnic Studies, 2007.

Obeysekere, Gananath. *The Cult of Goddess Pattini*. Chicago: University of Chicago Press, 1984.

Pfaffenberger, Bryan. *Caste in Tamil Culture: The Religious Foundations of Sudra Domination in Tamil Sri Lanka.* (Foreign and Comparative Studies, South Asian Series No. 7.) New York: Syracuse University, 1982.

Rajan, Somasundaram, Daya Sritharan K. and Rajani Thiranagama. *The Broken Palmyra, The Tamil Crisis in Sri Lanka: An Inside Account.* Jaffna: The Sri Lanka Studies Institute, Jaffna, 1990. (Second edition, 1992.)

Reeves, Peter, ed. *The Encyclopaedia of the Sri Lankan Diaspora.* Singapore: Editions Didier Millet, 2013.

Sivathamby, Karthigesu. *Sri Lankan Tamil Society and Politics.* Chennai: New Century Book House, 1995.

———. *Being a Tamil and Sri Lankan.* Colombo: Aivakam, 2006.

Somasundaram, Daya. *Scarred Communities: Psychological Impacts of Man-made and Natural Disasters on Sri Lankan Society.* New Delhi: Sage, 2014.

Subramanian, Samanth. *This Divided Island: Stories from the Sri Lankan War.* Gurgaon: Hamish Hamilton, Penguin Books, 2014.

Tambiah, Stanley. *Sri Lanka: Ethnic Fratricide and the Dismantling of Democracy.* Chicago: University of Chicago Press, 1986.

———. *Buddhism Betrayed? Religion, Politics, and Violence in Sri Lanka.* (A Monograph of the World Institute for Development Economics Research.) Chicago: University of Chicago Press, 1992.

Weiss, Gordon. *The Cage: The Fight for Sri Lanka and the Last Days of the Tamil Tigers.* London: The Bodley Head, 2011.

Whitaker, Mark P. *Amiable Incoherence: Manipulating Histories and Modernities in a Batticaloa Hindu Temple.* (Sri Lankan Studies Series.) Amsterdam: VU University Press, 1999.

———. *Learning Politics from Sivaram: The Life and Death of a Revolutionary Tamil Journalist in Sri Lanka.* London: Pluto Press, 2007.

Sri Lankan Tamil Literature

Cheran. *A Second Sunrise.* Edited and translated by Lakshmi Holmstrom and Sascha Ebeling. New Delhi: Navayana, 2012.

———. *In a Time of Burning.* Translated by Lakshmi Holmstrom. Lancs: Arc Publications, 2013.

Holmstrom, Lakshmi. Subashree Krishnaswamy, and K. Srilata, eds. *The Rapids of a Great River: The Penguin Book of Tamil Poetry*. New Delhi: Penguin Viking, 2009.

Kanganayakam, Chelva, ed. *Lutesong and Lament: Tamil Writing from Sri Lanka*. Toronto: TSAR, 2001.

———. *Wilting Laughter: Three Tamil Poets—Cheran, V.I.S. Jayapalan, Puthuvai Ratnathurai*. Translated by Chelva Kanganayakam. Toronto: TSAR, 2009.

———. Kanganayakam, Chelva, ed. & tr. *You Cannot Turn Away: Poems in Tamil by Cheran*. Translated by Chelva Kanganayakam. Toronto: TSAR, 2011.

———. *In Our Translated World: Contemporary Global Tamil Poetry*. Toronto: TSAR, 2013.

Malaravan. *War Journey: Diary of a Tamil Tiger*. Translated by N. Malathy. New Delhi: Penguin Books, 2013.

Muttulingam, A. *Inauspicious Times*. Translated by Padma Narayanan., Chennai: Indian Writing, 2008.

Neminathan, M., ed. *Tamil Ealam Literature: An Anthology*. London: Tamil Information Centre, 1996. (With an Introduction by Velupillai Prabhakaran.)

Ravikumar, ed. *Waking Is Another Dream: Poems on the Genocide in Eelam*. New Delhi: Navayana, 2010.

Selvadurai, Shyam, ed. *Many Roads through Paradise: An Anthology of Sri Lankan Literature*. New Delhi: Penguin Books, 2014.

Sivasegaram, S. *About Another Matter: Poems in Translation*. Colombo: Dhesiya Kalai Ilakkiya Peravai, 2004.

Shanaathanan, T. *The Incomplete Thompu*. Raking Leaves, 2011. (This is an interesting project on Art that engages with the destruction of the living environment in Jaffna, through maps, architectural sketches and paintings.)

Shanmugalingam. *Three Plays. Translated by S. Pathmanathan*. Colombo and Chennai: Kumaran Book House, 2007.

Shobasakthi. *Gorilla*. Translated by Anushiya Sivanarayanan. New Delhi: Random House, New Delhi, 2008.

———. *Traitor*. Translated by Anushiya Ramaswamy, Penguin Viking, New Delhi, 2010.

Subramanian, K.S., ed. & tr. *Tamil Poetry Today*. Chennai: International Institute of Tamil Studies, 2007.

Veluppillai, C. V. *In Ceylon's Tea Garden*. Talangama: Harrison Peiris for Ceylon Verse, 1956. (Second edition, Watagoda: Bakya Pathippagam, 2007.)

Wijesinha, Rajiva, ed. *Bridging Connections: An Anthology of Sri Lankan Short Stories*. New Delhi: National Book Trust, New Delhi, 2007.

Wijesinha, Rajiva, ed. *Mirrored Images: An Anthology of Sri Lankan Tamil Poetry*. New Delhi: National Book Trust, 2013.

Note: We have used the popular spellings for Tamil terms throughout this volume so as to facilitate the pronunciation and to make it easier for readers to search for Tamil resources on the Internet.

The French Institute of Pondicherry

The French Institute of Pondicherry (IFP), UMIFRE 21 CNRS-MAEE, is a financially autonomous institution under the joint authority of the French Ministry of Foreign and European Affairs (MAEE) and the French National Centre for Scientific Research (CNRS). It is a part of the network of twenty-seven research centres under this Ministry. It also forms part of the research unit 3330 'Savoirs et Mondes Indiens' of the CNRS, along with the Centre de Sciences Humaines (CSH) in New Delhi. It fulfils its missions of research, expertise and training in Human and Social Sciences and Ecology in South and Southeast Asia. It works particularly in the fields of Indian cultural knowledge and heritage (Sanskrit language and literature, history of religions, Tamil studies, etc.), contemporary social dynamics and the natural ecosystems of South India.

French Institute of Pondicherry, 11, St Louis Street, PB 33, Pondicherry 605001-India, Tel: (91) (413) 2231609, Email : ifpcom@ifpindia.org

Website: http: / / www.ifpindia.org